Keep 'Em Talking!

Real-Life Dilemmas That Teach

Keep 'Em Talking!

Real-Life Dilemmas That Teach

Mike Yaconelli

Youth Specialties

ZondervanPublishingHouse

Grand Rapids, Michigan

A Division of HarperCollinsPublishers

Keep 'Em Talking! Real-Life Dilemmas That Teach

© 1997 by Youth Specialties, Inc.

Youth Specialties Books, 1224 Greenfield Dr., El Cajon, CA 92021, are published by Zondervan Publishing House, 5300 Patterson Ave. S.E., Grand Rapids, MI 49530.

Library of Congress Cataloging-in-Publication Data

Yaconelli, Mike.
   Keep 'em talking! : real-life dilemmas that teach / Mike Yaconelli.
       p.   cm.
    Includes index.
    ISBN 0-310-21786-5
    1. Teenagers—Conduct of life—Problems, exercises, etc. 2. Christian ethics—Problems,
excercises, etc. 3. Church group work with teenagers. I. Title.
BJ1661.Y33   1997
268'.433—dc21   97-13787
                                                       CIP

Edited by Sheri Stanley
Cover and interior design by Michael Kern Design
Cover photo by Rob Gage – FPG International

Printed in the United States of America

98 99 00 01/ /4

CONTENTS

Sexuality

*Tess was a devout Christian, active in
her youth group—and pregnant.*

Parents & Family

*Cleaning out her daughter's closet,
Michelle's mom discovered her diary. Her
curiosity overcame her better judgment.*

Personal Spirituality

*"I asked God to make my mom
come to her senses. Nothing. I stopped
going to church. What's the point? God's
absence is so loud. He just disappeared."*

Truth & Deception

*It was the most amazing stereo system he'd ever seen—but
for $50? He knew it had to be stolen. But if he didn't ask
then he didn't technically know it was stolen, right?*

Poverty

*With a Haitian infant dead in her arms, Lisa
vowed her life to relieving hunger wherever
she could. Then she returned home...and it was
three months later while Christmas shopping
before she thought again of her promise.*

Racism

*"It's one thing to have black people in our church," Sophia's
father explained. "It's another thing to have them in your
family. You and he live in completely different cultures."*

Death & Dying

*After her leukemia diagnosis, Klarissa knew she
was a marked girl. It's not the leukemia, she thought,
but the terror of being alone that's killing me.*

...and More

*"They just don't want you coming to youth
group anymore. They think you're a bad influence."
"Why? Because I smoke?"
"And the way you dress. And some of your language."*

Alphabetical list of all dilemmas

All about simulated dilemmas, creative tension— and how to use *Keep 'Em Talking!*

Keep 'Em Talking! does just that—keeps kids talking. It's designed specifically to generate and energize discussions through simulated, real-life dilemmas. What you can do with this book is create opportunities for young people to understand how their faith works within the complex realities of everyday life.

Virtual Complexity

The dilemmas in *Keep 'Em Talking!* create a virtual reality of discussion generators. Each dilemma is designed to stimulate discussion around the kind of real-life tension that most decision making requires. So because most of the significant decisions we make in life are made in the crossfire of conflicting values, the discussions generated here are full of electricity and passion. Each dilemma brings young people to the place where they do their best to take stock of their motives and values—then decide not what they *should* do in a given situation, but what they *would* do.

Faith in Christ hardly simplifies some decisions, but rather makes them more difficult. Adding God into the decision-making mix, young people discover, seldom makes the "right" choice a clear one.

Each of these dilemmas is based on the author's three decades of working with teenagers. The situations are textured, complex, and realistic—the perfect testing ground for young people's faith. No discussion is easy—especially on such gritty subjects—but the dilemmas in *Keep 'Em Talking!* can make discussions easier.

High schoolers are at the age where they begin to understand how faith in Christ hardly simplifies some decisions, but rather makes them more difficult. Adding God into the decision-making mix, young people discover, seldom makes the "right" choice a clear one. But seeking God's voice can be invigorating and exciting, and adolescents are motivated to hear the whisper of God or see his fingerprint in the choices they make.

Built-In Energy

Tension is the natural electricity that results when faith and reality clash, when conflicting values meet, when hard choices must be made in the trenches of broken lives. And tension is what each dilemma in *Keep 'Em Talking!* purposely creates. If you believe in God, if you've decided to follow Christ wherever he leads, then *all* your decisions are at odds with prevailing cultural values. Moments of such decisions are filled with signif-

icance. Because faith matters, your decisions matter—and when there is much at stake, there is a resulting urgency or energy during the decision making. Faith adds suspense to each moment of our lives—and mystery can be a great catalyst for discussion.

The dilemmas in *Keep 'Em Talking!* create tension. Each strategy here has been included because of its potential to create a dilemma or situation with conflicting issues, which require young people to think through the alternatives and consequences before arriving at a decision. Tension is created when values overlap, making a simple black-and-white response impossible. Most decisions in the real world require sifting through layers of values before a choice is made.

For example, say a girl is asked to lie for a friend so the friend can be with her boyfriend. The girl is torn between her friendship, her respect for her friend's parents, telling the truth, and making it possible for her friend to lie. Diagramming this scenario could look like this:

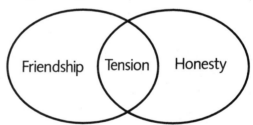

Where these values overlap, you'll find tension. A decision must be made—a decision that favors one value at the expense of other, often equally weighted values. The question is usually not *Which value is the right or wrong value?* but rather *Which value will have the priority alongside all the other values?*

Not only does such simulated tension help young people deliberately think through their day-to-day values, but it can also create an atmosphere of growth. Somewhere teenagers (particularly churched teenagers—not to mention churched adults) have picked up the idea that church is where you learn all the right answers. Of course the Christian faith provides a foundation upon which young people can deal with the particulars of life. But they must learn how to weigh and decide those particulars themselves.

For that reason, the discussions in this book do

not provide answers, but rather pose questions—healthy questions that cause growth.

Healthy Openness

There is no growth without an atmosphere of openness. That doesn't mean that the leader is always neutral, but that the leader is willing to let all points of view be at least aired without criticism. You don't teach children to ride a bicycle by criticizing them when they fall. You encourage, help, and show lots of patience. When young people are trying to figure out what life and faith are all about, they need to be encouraged and affirmed, not immediately corrected. They need to feel safe in their learning.

Safe environments—the kind that foster rewarding discussions among teenagers—are characterized by at least three characteristics:

• **Open-ended discussion.** Never bulldoze your group toward a conclusion. Of course, the group should stay focused on the subject, but don't feel that you must resolve all loose ends in 45 minutes. Discussion is squelched when young people feel pressured to resolve all issues. To the contrary, the emphasis ought to be on arriving at as many options as possible—so that when the decision is made, it is made with all the options (even "wrong" ones) clearly understood.

• **Freedom to say what you think.** Young people often feel penalized if they say what they really think—especially if what they think disagrees with the public position of a church or church leader. Small wonder that adolescents are reluctant to express their actual feelings, or even carefully think through all their options. Just remember that giving your students the space to say whatever it is they believe does not imply that you either agree or disagree with their ideas. It simply means that you approve of their right to introduce their ideas into the arena of discussion.

• **Learning as a laboratory.** Of all people, teenagers are the most inclined to think out loud, experiment with different options, try on exotic ideas, and see how they fit. So because your students merely verbalize a particular point of view does not mean they're investing any real belief in it. Let your discussions be laboratories where young people can freely experiment with any and all ideas.

Recreating the Realities of Life

If you want to provoke discussion through real-life dilemmas, you need three ingredients: ordinary people, realistic people, and confusing consequences.

• **Ordinary people.** It's easier for a young person to defend "Chris" than defend their own personal beliefs, for they don't feel threatened when discussing someone else's beliefs. Yet understand that when they talk about "Chris," they are likely telling you what *they* believe. Through a story about someone else, they may actually be expressing their own value system.

• **Realistic people.** Each of the human players in *Keep 'Em Talking!* is a mix of good and bad qualities—a thorough enough mix, as in real life, to usually make it impossible to find a good guy and a bad guy. Perfect people—and perfectly bad people—make it easy to decide who's right. But the people in this book, like the people you know, are flawed—a mix of good and bad traits.

Perfect people—and perfectly bad people—make it easy to decide who's right. But real people, like the people you know, are flawed—a mix of good and bad traits.

• **Confusing consequences.** As in real life, the consequences of our decisions can be as mixed as our motives. Suppose a girl chooses not to have sex with her boyfriend, whom she loves. She senses God's pleasure with her decision—and her boyfriend's displeasure and eventual departure. One consequence is good, another is painful.

How to Use *Keep 'Em Talking!*

Keep 'Em Talking! isn't a book of quickie lessons that will keep your students busy for an hour. Yet these 60 dilemmas can serve a variety of youth ministry needs:

As discussion starters

The whole point of *Keep 'Em Talking!* is to create lively discussion. Each dilemma is really a story, and almost all of them are set in commonplace situations just like those your young people live in. So you can count on the interest level being high. For example, rather than begin your meeting with the question, "What do you think about lying for a friend?" instead start with a story about Lisa, who asks her friend to lie for her because her parents are paranoid about Lisa's boyfriend. *Everyone* in your youth group will have an opinion about what should be done.

As a spiritual thermometer

You introduce a dilemma from *Keep 'Em Talking!*, you watch the discussion unfold—and soon you can observe just what it is that your students believe in. And since you're taking in the entire process of decision making, you know how they got to their beliefs. In other words, you'll know not only their values, but the premises of their values. This is helpful information for youth leaders who want to navigate their students into wiser decisions. If the content of your program is based on the needs of your students, *Keep 'Em Talking!* will become an integral part of your program.

As creative alternatives

You don't have to use *Keep 'Em Talking!* for only starting discussions. Use them to introduce (or debrief) a role play, to stimulate creative writing, to set the scene for a skit or dramatic situation. The possibilities are endless once kids are motivated and interested in a topic.

As tangents

The dilemmas in this book will almost always generate tangential issues. Because these strategies deal with many different values at the same time, you'll often find your young people talking about something that has nothing to do with your topic. What's happened is that, in the process of the discussion , they've found the central issue to them. Sometimes you'll need to gently lead them back onto your topic, but more often than not you'll want to pursue the "tangent," for it touches a need among your kids that you may not have noticed.

Don't fall for the prime-time TV myth that every conflict should be resolved within 55 minutes. Let your students go home still chewing on the problem.

P.S. Use *Keep 'Em Talking!* Carefully

Some cautionary remarks:

• **Let your knowledge of your kids dictate your programming.** Some young people aren't ready to handle some problems. You may want to discuss death—but because a parent of one of your students is dying, it may not be the time to discuss that subject. Then again, it may be the perfect time. Only you can make that decision because you know your kids.

• **Never let your kids forget that, despite life's ambiguities, there's still solid ground.** There's a lot of gray area and uncertainties out there, but there is also a lot

of positive content. Make sure your students get both. Generally, the more mature they get, the better they can handle ethical tensions and ambiguities.

• **Don't try to shock kids for effect.** If you play the devil's advocate, make sure your arguments are sensible. In other words, don't become so artificial in your role as spoiler that kids don't take your point of view seriously. If you try to shock kids with extreme arguments or positions, more often than not you'll create exactly what you don't want: your students will laugh off the discussion as they would a frivolous skit.

• **The dilemmas in *Keep 'Em Talking!* work best in small groups.** Divide your youth group into smaller groups of four to six kids. Each group's leader may be a student or adult. The leader should function as a facilitator, not a teacher. The goal of the small groups is to reach consensus—and if they can't, then to present the majority and the minority opinions to the entire group.

• **Give people time.** Don't fall for the prime-time TV myth that every conflict should be resolved within 55 minutes. Let your students go home still chewing on the problem. Sometimes let issues stay unresolved. It takes time to think through difficult questions. When young people leave the youth group with unresolved issues, they usually end up talking with someone about them—like parents or friends. And that's exactly the kind of dialogue you want to create (even though you aren't there to hear it).

• **Don't be afraid of controversy or failure.** When you create tension or tackle controversial issues, you'll generate criticism from students as well as from their parents. Sometimes the criticism will be justified because you've made a mistake. Sometimes you'll even lose a young person. But such are the risks of good teaching. Admit your mistakes, learn from your failures—but don't back off simply because you've pushed people into new areas of growth and maturity.

Pregnancy Test

She stared at the stick. How could she be pregnant? She had broken up with Don a month ago, and they had made only that one mistake… and what a mistake it was turning out to be.

Tess was a devout Christian, active in her youth group, and deeply committed to her faith. So were her parents. Everyone had warned her that she and Don were getting too serious, but Tess ignored them. Until the mistake, that is—and then she immediately broke up with Don and prayed hard that she wouldn't get pregnant. Apparently she hadn't prayed hard enough.

Tess was against abortion—but when Jennifer, her best friend, gave her the card of an abortion clinic, she took it.

"Tess, your parents would be crushed if they found out you were pregnant," Jennifer said. "Their lives would be ruined, and so would yours. You can get an abortion and no one will know. Think about Don, think about your future. You're not ready to have a baby. You're 17. Do it, Tess. That way no one gets hurt."

A few days later Tess's mom walked into her daughter's room. "What's this?" she asked. She held a business card from the local Planned Parenthood chapter. "Are you pregnant?"

"Mom, where did you get that card? Did you go through my purse again?"

"It doesn't matter where or how I got this, Tess. All I want to know is if you're pregnant."

"It matters a lot if you look in my purse without asking! Since you want to know, yes, I'm pregnant!"

The silence was deafening. Finally, quietly, her mom spoke.

"What are you going to do?"

"I don't know what I'm going to do. I told Don, and Don told me to get an abortion. He doesn't want anything to do with me or the baby. I don't believe in abortion, and I know how strongly you and Dad are against it, but I don't think I can go through with a pregnancy. If I'm going to make it, Mom, I'm going to need your help, not your anger."

Her mother took Tess in her arms. "Tess, we'll handle it. No one will know. We'll find a good doctor to do the abortion… out of the area."

Tess couldn't believe what she had heard. "What? You want me to have an abortion? So I guess abortion is wrong for everyone else?" she asked bitterly.

"That's not true, Tess. We still believe abortion is wrong, but sometimes there can be things more wrong than abortion."

"Yeah, I see what you mean. What's more wrong than abortion is having your wonderful Christian friends find out that your perfect Christian daughter is pregnant."

"It's bad enough

to make one mistake. But you shouldn't make two mistakes. Okay, so I got a girl pregnant. But I don't want to raise a kid. I don't have any money and neither does my girlfriend. So it's better to bring a baby into the world that isn't wanted? I don't think so. I'm only a sophomore. I can't get a job anyway. Abortion is the only alternative."

Dennis, 16, a sophomore

The Stats

- According to the Alan Guttmacher Institute, approximately 22 million legal abortions were reported in 1987.

- It is estimated that between four and nine million were not reported, for a possible total of 26 to 31 million legal abortions.

- Add to that an estimated 10 to 22 million "clandestine" abortions, and the total worldwide figure is between 36 and 53 million abortions.

- China reports the highest number of abortions, with 10,394,500 reported in 1987. Women in the former Soviet Union have the highest rate of abortion…181 abortions per 1,000 women aged 15-44 in 1987, or roughly 60 percent of all pregnancies ending in abortion.

- The average Russian woman has three to eight abortions in her lifetime. The rate of abortion in Russia is four times higher than that of the U.S. There is a worldwide trend toward liberalizing abortion laws.

International Family Planning Perspectives, **June 1990;** *USA Today,* **August 8, 1996**

By the Book…

Be careful not to do your "acts of righteousness" before men, to be seen by them. If you do, you will have no reward from your Father in heaven.

Matthew 6:1

---

1. Rank the characters from best to worst: Tess, Don, Jennifer, Tess's mom.
   best _____
   _____
   _____
   worst _____

2. What would you do if you were Tess?

3. What would you do if you were Don?

4. What are Tess's options?

"My boyfriend

gave me an STD. He didn't even know he had it. Now I have to go through the humiliation of treatment. Whatever girl he was involved with was an idiot. Why didn't she tell him? She must have known."

16-year-old sophomore girl

The Stats

✪ Every year 2.5 million U.S. teenagers get STDs. When teenagers have sex at a young age, they are unaware of using contraception. Girls are embarrassed to ask their boyfriends to use a condom. This is one of the reasons why teens are two to three times more likely to contract STDs than people over 20 years old.

For Teens Only
May 6, 1996

✪ Of 12 million cases of STDs diagnosed every year, three million occur in teens, according to the Institute of Medicine in Washington.

Unfortunately, for every dollar the government spends on STD prevention, it shells out $43 treating them. That's $10 billion a year, not including the money spent on AIDS.

Another survey found that one in 10 Americans can't even name a STD, while only about a quarter know about, for example, chlamydia—the most common STD—which strikes four million Americans annually.

Chicago Tribune
November 20, 1996

By the Book...

Do not judge, or you too will be judged. For in the same way you judge others, you will be judged, and with the measure you use, it will be measured to you.
Matthew 7:1

All men are liars...
Psalm 116:11

WHEN EXPERIENCE MATTERS

Herpes? Ross had genital herpes? Darcie couldn't believe what she was hearing. Ross, a college sophomore, was the president of the college youth group and two years older than Darcie. He was the most wonderful guy she had ever known. They had been going together for a month, and after hours of talking Darcie thought she knew everything about Ross. They were both Christians, and Ross was planning on going to seminary. As far as Darcie was concerned, she had met the man of her dreams.

But the dream was turning into a nightmare.

Darcie heard herself ask the unthinkable. "How did you get herpes, Ross?"

"Well, I've only been a Christian for a year, Darc," he explained, "and before that I was a pretty wild guy. Lots of drinking. I even dabbled in drugs for a while. Let's put it this way—I was involved with a lot of girls before I met you. I'm not proud of my past. I didn't want you to know. But when this herpes thing flared up, I thought I had better tell you."

Darcie was more upset than she expected. "If he has herpes, what other diseases is he carrying?" The thought of Ross with other girls turned her stomach. Darcie was a virgin and expected the guys she dated to be virgins.

"Ross," she said "I'm sorry, but I can't go on in this relationship. I know God has forgiven you, and I don't consider you bad or anything…it's just that I want to marry someone who hasn't been with other girls."

It seemed that Ross took the news well. He apologized for not telling her at the beginning of their relationship and even asked her to pray with him.

A month later Darcie found out from a friend that Ross had been telling everyone that Darcie thought she was too good for Ross. According to Ross, Darcie told him he was tainted goods and that even though God had forgiven him, she couldn't.

1. What are Darcie's options?

2. Do you agree with Darcie's decision about Ross?

3. If God forgives someone's past, shouldn't we?

4. If you were Darcie, what would you have done when you found out about Ross's past?

The Fear of Sex

No one would have suspected that deep inside the mind of Chip Davis were serious doubts about sex. Chip, a junior, was the most eligible guy in school. Truth was, Chip didn't have a girlfriend, hardly ever dated, and secretly didn't want to go out at all.

Why? He was afraid of sex.

He was pretty sure the only time his parents had sex was before he was born. He had heard them fighting about sex many times, and he knew it was the source of their marital problems. Of course, Chip went to movies like everyone else, but those love scenes were so intimidating to him. All the perfect bodies and perfect lovemaking. He knew that many of the actors and actresses used body doubles because their perfect bodies were not perfect enough. He knew from his friends that many of their sexual experiences were not fun—sex in the back of a car, sex at their girlfriend's house—rushed and just not that satisfying.

Chip felt like he was a normal guy with normal impulses. It was just that sex was a scary problem to him. It wasn't the moral stuff, although he was beginning to think there were some pretty good reasons why a person should wait until marriage. What bothered him most was the comparison part, the competition part. Would he be as good as the last guy? Would she compare him to someone else? Shouldn't there be more to a relationship than sex? Chip felt weird, like he was some strange kind of guy for worrying like this about sex. In fact, he wondered sometimes if there was something wrong with him—if he was gay.

But I like girls, he thought. I want to spend time with them, get to know them, be friends with them, laugh with them, have fun together—without all the sexual pressure. I just want to go out on a date, not make out all night. I want to write notes, buy her gifts, talk all night. Is there something wrong with that? With me?

1. Is there something wrong with Chip?

2. What kind of sexual pressures do you experience at school?

3. How do you cope with sexual pressure?

4. If a person publicly suggested at school that sex is not all everyone says it is, would that person be criticized? Ridiculed? Accused of being gay?

"Hey, I'm not weird.
I like a good-looking girl as much as anyone else. I mean, I'm going with Jennifer, the all-time best-looking girl in our high school. She has a great body. But I'm not going with her just because of her body. It's her I like. I don't want to have sex—I just want to be with her. All my friends say I'm lying. Well, they're wrong—and that's why Jennifer likes me. She knows I'm not going with her for the sex."

Zane, 18

The Stats

- 61% of girls and 23% of boys cite sexual pressure from dating partners.
- 59% of girls and 51% of boys say they had sex because they thought they were ready.
- 45% of girls have sex because they equate it with love; 28% of boys use that reason.
- 38% of girls are afraid of getting labeled a virgin; 43% of boys fear that label.

Youthworker Update
August 1996

By the Book...

Now for the matters you wrote about: It is good for a man not to marry.
1 Corinthians 7:1

Flee from sexual immorality. All other sins a man commits are outside his body, but he who sins sexually sins against his own body.

1 Corinthians 6:18

"Birth control

can be dangerous, unnecessary, and sex-inhibiting. If you can't control your sexual desire then stay away from the opposite sex. If you want to have a boyfriend or a girlfriend then you should be mature enough to know how to stop. Besides, oral sex is just as fun, and you don't have to worry about getting pregnant."

19-year-old male

"Nobody waits until they're married to have sex anymore. Nobody. Sure, you have to be careful—but having sex is a normal part of modern relationships".

Jean, 17, church youth group president

The Stats

PROTECTION AGAINST PREGNANCY

Method of birth control	Effectiveness if used perfectly all the time	Effectiveness based on surveys of couples who used the method
◻ **Pill** (combined with estrogen and progestin)	99%	92%
◻ **IUD** (intrauterine device)	98%	92%
◻ **Condoms**	97%	90%
◻ **Foam, suppositories** (spermicides)	97%	75%
◻ **Condoms and foam**	99%	95%
◻ **Diaphragm**	97%	80%
◻ **Rhythm** (calendar)	85%	60%-75%
◻ **No method** (hope)	10%	10%

Washington University Student Health Service, February 1996

By the Book...

Do you not know that the wicked will not inherit the kingdom of God? Do not be deceived: Neither the sexually immoral nor idolaters or adulterers nor male prostitutes nor homosexual offenders nor thieves nor the greedy nor drunkards nor slanderers nor swindlers will inherit the Kingdom of God.

1 Corinthians 6:9-10

BIRTH-CONTROL BUST

Robin didn't sleep around. Sure, she was planning on sleeping with her boyfriend, but that wasn't "sleeping around." She loved her boyfriend and they planned on getting married. She was 18 and old enough to make her own decisions.

So when Robin finally decided it was time to have sex, she went to a health clinic for birth-control pills. What Robin didn't know was that a clinic nurse was a good friend of her mom's.

When Robin got home from the clinic, she had quite a surprise waiting for her.

"Sit down," her mother said harshly. "I understand you purchased birth-control pills."

Robin was caught off guard. "Well, Mom, since I'm eighteen—"

"Since I'm still paying all the bills around here," her mother interrupted, "let me explain how it works in our house. As long as I'm paying for your food, your car, and your insurance, and as long as you are staying in my house, you will live by my values. I thought I raised you to believe in Christian values. I thought you were a Christian. Apparently you have decided to love your boyfriend more than God, more than your parents, and I guess I can't stop you. But I can stop you from taking birth-control pills.

"So you have a choice. You can choose to have a sexual relationship with Toby—and get your own apartment, your own job, and pay for all of your own expenses. Or you can promise me you and Toby will not have a sexual relationship, you will not purchase birth-control pills, and you will live by the values of your father and Me. It's up to you."

The conversation went well into the night, but in the end Robin agreed to give up the birth-control pills, refrain from a sexual relationship with Toby, and live by her mom and dad's rules. What else could she do, she thought? So she promised there'd be no sex.

Her mother never found out that Robin soon became sexually active with Toby and, three months later, had an abortion. She graduated from high school, broke up with Toby, went to a Christian college, and met a Christian boy. Her parents were very proud of her.

1. Do you agree that if your parents pay the bills, they have the right to demand that you live by their values?

2. What options did Robin have?

3. Does everyone have secrets their parents will never know? Do you? Is it actually better for parents to not know everything?

4. If Robin had come to you after her discussion with her mother, what advice would you have given her?

Church Affair

Christian Community Church was one of the largest in the city—nearly 4,000 people attended, with 500 kids coming to youth group each week. Angie had become a Christian her junior year and was one of the most active kids in the church. Every week she was at youth group, Bible study, discipleship group, and the leadership planning meeting.

Angie's parents, however, didn't attend church when she first started going. Their marriage wasn't doing well. After lots of prayer from the youth group, Angie's mom finally agreed to come to church—and she even liked it. After a few months her mother had even gone to the pastor for counseling, and it looked like the marriage was doing better, too.

Angie's life had genuinely changed after her conversion. She broke up with a long-time boyfriend with whom she was sexually active and became a strong voice in the youth group for sexual abstinence. Christ had really changed her life, and it looked like he was changing her parents' lives as well. Angie was happy with where her life was going. Christianity really did change her life for the better.

Until one night when Angie arrived at youth group. All the kids were talking. They looked worried, some of the girls were crying, and some of the guys were angry.

"What's going on?" Angie asked.

"You haven't heard? Pastor Daniels has been having an affair and had to leave the church. Everyone's talking about it."

Angie couldn't believe it. Not Pastor Daniels. He was a great pastor. His sermons were really interesting—and funny. Sure, he was kind of attractive, but he had a wonderful family. In fact, Angie was good friends with one of his daughters. He had just given a four-week series on the Christian view of sex, which had really helped Angie. No, this just couldn't be. The information had to be wrong.

"He resigned voluntarily. He admitted he was having an affair."

Angie didn't know how to respond. She felt betrayed. Youth group was a shambles that night, so Angie left before the meeting was over. When she arrived home, her mother was upset and had been crying.

"Angie, I...I need to talk to you. Pastor Daniels resigned from the church tonight."

"I know, Mom. Everyone knows. That's all we talked about at youth group. I guess he was having an affair. He admitted it."

"He was having an affair with *me.*"

At first her mother's words seemed a blur. Angie felt dizzy, nauseated. Her brain hadn't registered what her body already understood. All Angie knew was that she would rather be dead than hear what she just heard. It was too much, the betrayal too deep, reality too hard. Life would be impossible to live with this knowledge. Her own mother involved with a minister she had loved and trusted. Her own mother.

Angie never went back to church. Any church. She refused to talk with any kids in the youth group. Her parents got a divorce, and Angie never trusted anyone again. Who could blame her?

1. What would you have said to Angie when she found out about her mother? On the back write Angie a letter

2. Would you have been able to defend Christianity after what happened?

3. If you were Angie, what would you have done?

4. What could the youth group have done for Angie?

"When it comes to sex,
how can Christian people even show their faces? They are so screwed up it's unbelievable. How many TV evangelists and ministers and youth directors have been caught having sex with a hooker or someone in their church? Christians are such hypocrites. They keep telling everyone else to wait until marriage, while they're having sex like rabbits. Forget them."

17-year-old senior male

The Stats

According to a study by Tom W. Smith of the National Opinion Research Center, roughly 15% of married or previously married Americans have committed adultery. The results largely agree with the 1987 ABC News/Washington Post poll that found 89% of spouses faithful. Other pop culture gurus, on the other hand, have stoked reports of rampant infidelity: Kinsey says 37% percent of men have committed adultery; Joyce Brothers, 50% of women; and Shere Hite, 75% of women married 5 years.

Family Research Council
Washington Watch
October 29, 1993

By the Book...

It is actually reported that there is sexual immorality among you, and of a kind that does not occur even among pagans...Hand this man over to Satan, so that the sinful nature may be destroyed and his spirit saved on the day of the Lord.

1 Corinthians 5:1, 5

Now instead, you ought to forgive and comfort him, so that he will not be overwhelmed by excessive sorrow. I urge you, therefore, to reaffirm your love for him.

2 Corinthians 2: 7-8

"Any person who sexually abuses a child should do five years of mandatory prison time. I don't care if the abuser is your father, mother, or grandparent. Sexual abusers are the worst kind of criminal."

Linda, high school senior

The Stats

One of every three girls and one of every four to six boys are sexually assaulted at least once before the age of 18. More than 85% of child sexual assault victims are abused by someone they know and trust. The average time a child remains the victim of incest is seven years.

**The Kentucky Child Assault
Prevention (CAP) Project
February 13, 1996**

By the Book...

Do not have sexual relations with your son's daughter or your daughter's daughter; that would dishonor you...Everyone who does any of these detestable things—such persons must be cut off from their people.

Leviticus 18:10, 29

JAN'S TERRIBLE SECRET

J an is outgoing and cute, with lots of friends. She dates occasionally, but seems to be more comfortable with her girlfriends than with guys.

Jan and her best friend, Linda, decide to go with several others from their school to a Young Life week-long summer camp. As the week progresses, they not only have fun, but get to know each other better than ever.

One night during cabin talk, Jan doesn't join the conversation. She just sits there, staring into space. Suddenly she starts to cry uncontrollably and runs from the cabin. Linda has no idea what's wrong with her friend, but follows her out. When Jan stops running, Linda catches up with her and comforts her until the crying subsides. Finally, Jan reveals the secret that has been killing her inside.

For the past eight years, Jan's grandfather has been sexually abusing her. He has threatened to kill her if she tells anyone. She feels scared, dirty, and sinful. She says she loves her grandfather—everyone loves him, and that's what makes it so difficult. She knows that if she tells her parents what has been happening, it will destroy them.

As they walk back to the cabin, Jan makes Linda promise to keep this a secret.

1. What are Linda's options?

2. What are Jan's options?

3. If you decided to keep Jan's secret with her, what could you do to help?

4. If you are asked to keep information secret, when someone is being seriously harmed, are you bound to your promise?

DATE RAPE DILEMMA

Tammy is a very attractive 17-year-old junior, with plenty of guys always wanting to go out with her. Her latest boyfriend is Reggie, an 18-year-old senior—and a stud. The first few dates were great, but the last one was more like a wrestling match. Tammy was used to wrestling with guys over sex, but it usually happened only once and then the guy got the message.

Reggie was different. He kept pushing. And Tammy kept resisting. But the night came when Reggie wouldn't take "no" for an answer, and Tammy gave up. It devastated her. Not only did she feel guilty for giving in, she blamed herself. She should have called for help, but the truth is that in the heat of the moment, she was confused. She immediately broke off the relationship with Reggie and kept it all to herself. Her shame kept her from telling even her closest friend.

Days went by and the incident continued to haunt her. Then she saw a TV show on date rape and realized that's what had happened to her—Reggie had raped her. If a guy has sex with you while you are saying no in unmistakable terms, it's date rape.

So Tammy confronted Reggie—and he got upset.

"Date rape? Come on, Tammy, you wanted it just as badly as I did. Have you forgotten what you were wearing that night?" As a matter of fact, Tammy had forgotten—she was wearing skin-tight leggings and a mini-top that exposed her midriff.

"It doesn't matter what I was wearing, Reggie. I kept telling you no, and you wouldn't stop."

Reggie got madder. "Yeah, but you didn't scream or freak out or try and get away. Sure, you said no, but it was obvious you meant yes."

Tammy was still convinced that she had been raped. She got an appointment with a lawyer, a friend of the family. The lawyer was sympathetic, but she warned Tammy that the process wouldn't be easy—and would probably get ugly. The lawyer pointed out that Tammy hadn't reported the date rape to the police, hadn't told anyone about it, there were no physical signs of a struggle, and the clothes she was wearing did sound as if they were provocative. None of these details justified what Reggie did, the lawyer admitted, but Reggie nevertheless stood a good chance of winning the case. And even if Tammy won, her reputation could be ruined by the publicity.

But Tammy can't let it go. She was raped, forced to have sex against her will, and she doesn't want Reggie to get away with what he did. What he did was wrong! Tammy knows the odds are stacked against her. And she knows she has a reputation as a flirt, even among the kids in her youth group. Tammy doesn't know where to turn or what to do.

"What a joke!

These days everything is date rape! Look out, man—if you're a guy, it's open season on us. All a girl needs to do to get back at you for breaking up with her is start screaming "Date rape!" I don't think date rape is a problem at all. I think it's just a bunch of feminists getting back at the men they hate."

20-year-old college male

The Stats

15% of female college students become victims of rape, and a further 11% become targets of attempted rape, according to a national survey undertaken in 1985 by Mary P. Koss (professor of psychology at the University of Arizona). Koss also found that 84% of the women who had been raped knew their assailants, 57% of the incidents had occurred during dates, and 73% of the assailants and 55% of the victims had used alcohol or other drugs prior to the assault.

Sexual Assault Information
Internet page
February 20, 1997

By the Book...

Can a man scoop fire into his lap without his clothes being burned? Can a man walk on hot coals without his feet being scorched?

Proverbs 6:27, 28

1. What are Tammy's options?

2. Who was more responsible for having sex, Reggie or Tammy?

3. What would you advise Tammy to do?

4. Is there a Christian response to this situation?

5. What would you do if you were Tammy? If you were Reggie?

?

The Weaker Sex

"Girls are always talking about hunks. Always a new heartthrob they all salivate over. They have to have the latest underwear or nightgown from Victoria's Secret, or the newest designer perfume, the tightest pants, and most revealing top. But when I make a move on a girl, she acts all offended. I know she'll go back to her girlfriends and say I'm a sex fiend. You know, I'll be honest—I actually like the opera. And I think it'd be a great date to spend the evening at Barnes & Noble reading some cool books over coffee. Yeah, right…if I invited some girl to Barnes & Noble, she'd be telling everyone I was gay."

Dan, 18

The Stats

Battle of the Sexes
By subject, who is better?

Course	Boys	Girls	About equal
Social studies/history	23%	21%	56%
Music	11	35	54
Science	34	14	52
Math	25	24	51
Art	26	26	48
English/writing	4	68	28
Foreign languages	7	44	49

By the Book...

Now to the unmarried and the widows I say: It is good for them to stay unmarried, as I am. But if they cannot control themselves, they should marry, for it is better to marry than to burn with passion.

1 Corinthians 7:8-9

A t two in the morning the slumber-party discussion turned (again) to guys, and this time all the girls were in agreement.

"Why are guys so boring? Why can't they plan dates that are fun? Why can't they plan at all?" The girls were having a field day comparing stories. Guys either asked them to go to a movie or to watch a video. Period. Those were the usual options. All other dates were part of the school schedule—football games, dances, the mandatory Friday night party.

"Why can't guys think of something creative—a picnic, a hike, a scavenger hunt, a cookout—or even cooking their own gourmet dinner?" The girls decided they knew why guys don't think of any creative dates: all they can think about is sex. They want to get the movie over with so they can get on with it—and sometimes they can 't even wait, and start making out there in the theater.

The girls talked about how wonderful it would be if you could spend an entire evening or day with a guy without him making one sexual move. Just to have fun or be with a guy without any sexual pressure would be so rare!

The girls decided on one other reason for guys' lack of creativity—they're afraid. Afraid to do something different, because other guys might criticize them—or worse yet, the date might not work. Guys really are wimps, the girls concluded—definitely the weaker sex.

1. Do you agree or disagree with the girls' conclusions?

2. Why don't guys plan creative dates?

3. Have you ever been on a creative date?

4. Do you agree with the girls that sex is the motivation for most guys?

The Sexual Solution

Mark and Tina had been going steady for almost two years now. He's a senior, she's a junior. They were both active in their church's youth group and in the local Young Life meetings, so they spent a lot of time together. But lately their relationship hadn't been going well.

"I know the answer," Lori advised Tina. "Sex. Believe, me it will strengthen your relationship." Lori had been in a similar dilemma with her boyfriend: when their one-year-old relationship became shaky, sex seemed to bring the two of them closer together. The sexual solution worked for them.

Tina was surprised that such a solution was suggested by a couple in her youth group. Tina had just assumed that everyone in her youth group believed in waiting until marriage. Actually, this was the second time someone had suggested it…Mark had been recommending the sexual solution for the past three months.

Tina sensed that if she didn't have sex with Mark soon, she'd lose him. She really wanted to wait until marriage, but guys like Mark didn't come along every day. She knew what her parents believed, she knew what the church believed, and she thought she knew what she believed. She was very confused.

But Tina finally decided. She loved Mark very much, and they agreed they were going to be married. Mark was the one guy for her. So she took Lori's advice—and it worked! After their sexual experience Mark and Tina did seem to be closer. For three months everything was wonderful.

Until the day that Mark told her that after graduation he was going to a college 3,000 miles away, and that he thought it would be best if he and Tina spent some time away from each other.

Tina was stunned. Just a few nights before, Mark was talking about attending a local junior college during Tina's senior year. Tina called Lori. Lori was clueless. She and her boyfriend were getting along fine.

"I had sex with this guy.

It wasn't great, but I still liked it. Anyway, I felt guilty about it and asked God to forgive me. I even broke up with the guy. My youth leader told me that God forgave me, but I should never do it again. I know she was right, but every time I go out with a new guy I want to [have sex]. I can't help it. Once you've experienced it, you can't exactly go back to holding hands. Anyone who thinks you can have sex, and then not have it anymore, is crazy."

Tina, 16, a junior

"Sex is a great relationship fixer. You feel close to the person and you forget what you were mad about. You don't have to be in love to have sex—God made it so people have a way of making each other feel good. That's cool. I've had sex with lots of people. Now I'm no slut, but I sure have made a lot of people happy. What's wrong with that?"

17-year-old junior, male

The Stats

Abstinence was the norm among unmarried American teenage girls at least until 1982, according to the National Survey of Family Growth. The best of the recent surveys of high school age youths (teens between 14 and 17 years old) was conducted as part of the National Health Interview Survey of 1992. This survey showed that 57% of adolescents were virgins. A series of surveys conducted over the last 25 years by Who's Who Among American High School Students shows that only one in four top students is sexually active.

The Heritage Foundation, August 31, 1995

By the Book...

So I say, live by the Spirit, and you will not gratify the desires of the sinful nature. For the sinful nature desires what is contrary to the Spirit, and the Spirit what is contrary to the sinful nature. They are in conflict with each other, so that you do not do what you want. The acts of the sinful nature are obvious: sexual immorality, impurity and debauchery;...I warn you, as I did before, that those who live like this will not inherit the kingdom of God.

Galatians 5:16-17, 19, 21

1. What do you think about a sexual solution to a shaky relationship?

2. What would you tell Tina if she had called you right after Mark had broken off the relationship?

3. Would you be surprised to discover that kids in your church youth group were having sex?

"I made a mistake

once. I was involved with a very destructive guy. He was much older than me, and I wouldn't listen to my parents or anyone else when they told me this guy was bad news. I admit it—it was a mistake. What I am trying to tell my parents is that mistakes teach you. They teach you more than any lecture or book. I learned my lesson. But will my parents understand? Not a chance. Instead of hearing me admit my mistake, they use it against me. They hold it over my head and are now paranoid about every person I go out with."

Becky, 16

The Stats

Who needs sex ed. in schools?

- ❑ A third of 12-to-18-year-olds say the media influenced their decisions to have sex, with more than half claiming their birth-control training came from TV or movies.

- ❑ A third of them also say they have sex because TV and movies make it seem normal.

- ❑ A third of the girls got their birth-control and STD info from fashion magazines.

- ❑ Three-fourths of teens said at least one parent talked to them about sex.

- ❑ Nearly half (46%) said parents talked to them about birth control.

From a survey by the Henry J. Kaiser Family Foundation, in
Youthworker Update, **September 1996**

By the Book...

The heart is deceitful above all things and beyond cure. Who can understand it?
Jeremiah 17:9

Likewise every good tree bears good fruit, but a bad tree bears bad fruit. A good tree cannot bear bad fruit, and a bad tree cannot bear good fruit. Every tree that does not bear good fruit is cut down and thrown into the fire. Thus, by their fruit you will recognize them.
Matthew 7:17-20

PROPHETIC PARENTS

Christa had dreamed about having a steady boyfriend for the first three years of high school—and now she had him. Terence was so cool…tall, good looking, athletic. The perfect guy, just the kind she'd like to marry. Okay, he was having some school problems (he was flunking two classes) and girl problems (he had been sexually involved with two other girls earlier in the year), but it had been a difficult year for him. His parents had split up for the umpteenth time, his mom lost her job, they had no money, and Terence had totaled his car after a party the first week of school. No wonder he was having some problems here and there.

Christa totally understood and tried to help him as much as possible. She helped him with his homework, loaned him money when he needed it, and drove him around in her car. In short, she fell hard for Terence. She wanted to spend every waking moment with him. This was no puppy-love, they told each other. It was the real thing.

Of course her parents didn't understand. They didn't like Terence, didn't trust him, and didn't think he was good for Christa. "He's going to hurt you, Christa," they warned her constantly. "He's a loser."

Their warnings made Christa go ballistic. "You don't know him! You don't know anything about him! You just don't want me to grow up. You think I'm too young for a serious relationship. Well, you're wrong!"

Christa and Terence saw each other every day for four months, even though her parents were always trying to slow them down, keep them apart, and warning of problems with trusting Terence. When Christa finally decided that Terence was the guy she was going to marry, she decided to become sexually active. She was so glad she did. She and Terence would be forever.

Christa never heard of chlamydia. All she knew is that every time she urinated it was painful, and there was some kind of discharge. The doctor at the free clinic told her chlamydia was a sexually transmitted disease. She was humiliated. When she asked Terence about it, he admitted that he knew he had the disease, but didn't want to tell her—and especially didn't want to tell her that he probably contracted while he and Christa were dating.

Her parents were right, Christa thought. How could Terence be such a creep? Christa broke up with him. It didn't matter to her what Terence had said: "Christa, please, I'm sorry, really sorry. You are just the kind of girl I've always wanted. I didn't realize what I had until now. Please take me back…I promise nothing like this will ever happen again."

1. What would you do if you were Christa?

2. Should Christa tell her parents about the chlamydia?

3. If you were Christa's parents and you found out about Terence giving your daughter an STD what would you do?

4. Do you think guys like Terence will ever change?

?

HOME ALONE

It's Friday night, and Sharon's boyfriend invites her to his house for pizza and a video. His parents are home, he tells Sharon and her parents. But when Sharon arrives, she finds out that Chuck's parents are not home and won't return until 11:00 that night. "Some of my parents' friends just showed up from out of town," he explains, "and they went to meet them at the airport."

Sharon knows she's not to be at a guy's house without his parents there, but it's already 8:00—and what can happen in three hours? So she decides to stay.

During the movie Chuck asks her what she wants to drink. Diet Coke, she says. Chuck disappears into the kitchen, and a few moments later plops down next to her again with a Diet Coke in one hand—and a beer in the other.

"Chuck, what are you doing?"

"Sharon, let's have a little fun tonight, okay?"

Now she's nervous. She doesn't want to stay, but neither does she want to lose her boyfriend over a legitimate change of plans and one can of beer. About the time that she decides to relax and enjoy the movie, she notices that Chuck has placed the remainder of a six-pack next to him. Now she's really worried, and doesn't know what to do.

1. What are Sharon's options?

2. What would you do?

3. It's obvious that Chuck knows his parents are supposed to be home. Is this another instance of a guy expecting the girl to say no?

4. What are Chuck's options?

5. What should Chuck have done?

The Stats

High school seniors who date spend 14½ hours a week alone with their dates. So how are they spending their date time?

- 86% hang out at home.
- 64% go out to eat.
- 63% go out to the movies.
- 63% make out.
- 59% watch TV.

USA Today
September 25, 1995

By the Book...

Do not get drunk on wine, which leads to debauchery. Instead, be filled with the Spirit.

Ephesians 5:18

"If we knew

what homosexuals actually do to each other, there wouldn't be a person in the world who would allow such behavior. It's not normal. I don't care whether they're attracted to each other or not, they have to learn how to control their urges just like everyone else. I have never understood why sexuality is so complicated. When you drop something, it falls to the ground. It doesn't fly. The law of gravity is pretty simple. So is the law of nature: A goes into B. When you try and make A go into C, it doesn't work."

Quentin, 19, youth minister

The Stats

Among parents of gay men hearing for the first time about their sons' sexual orientation, initial reaction was perceived as negative, with a general improvement in relationship over time. Upon initial disclosure by the sons, 55% of the mothers had negative reactions, while only 42% of the fathers had negative reactions.

This begins to dismantle the commonly held myth that gay men can expect their mothers to be more sympathetic to coming out than their fathers.

Phillips Graduate Institute, 1996

By the Book...

A friend loves at all times.

Proverbs 17:17a

NO SECRETS...ALMOST

Sara and Jon have been close friends since they were in kindergarten. Both have grown up in the church and are active in church, especially in youth choir. Sara knows more about Jon than about any of her friends—even her girlfriends. They have no secrets. Both Sara and Jon graduated from high school at the top of their class and have been accepted at prestigious universities.

Late one August night, just a week before they leave for school, Jon stops by and wants to talk. Sara suggests their favorite talking spot, where they both walk in the warm summer night. For a long time Jon is silent, and Sara knows something serious is bothering him.

"Sara, I'm doing more than going to college next week," he finally says. "I'm sharing a dorm room with a guy I met at a tennis tournament this year. I'm gay, Sara, and he is my lover. I'm sorry I never told you about this, but you're my best friend and I was afraid of what me being gay might do to your reputation. I didn't want to embarrass you. But since I'm coming out, sort of— I'm not telling my parents just yet—I owe it to you. But please don't tell anyone else until I get up enough courage to tell my parents. Can I count on you?"

Sara is stunned. The conflicting emotions are overwhelming—anger, shock, hurt, empathy, confusion, depression, fear. Sara was paralyzed about what to do. She doesn't know what to say, and instead finds herself crying.

?

1. Should Sara keep Jon's secret secret?

2. What if she sees Jon's parents? What about the kids at church and youth choir?

3. Is Jon fair to wait until this moment to tell Sara about his homosexuality?

4. Up until now Sara has always thought of herself as anti-gay, but now she doesn't know what to think. Jon is a Christian—or at least she thought so. Can a person be gay and a Christian?

5. What would you do?

Sexuality On Hold

Although he can't remember the exact moment the thought first crossed his mind, Jay wonders if he's gay. Oh, there was the normal exploratory stuff that guys do when they're growing up, but nothing out of the ordinary. He wasn't abused when he was a kid, but now that he's in high school, the wondering has become a serious concern.

What bothers Jay is having no serious relationships with girls. His friendships with girls have been just that—friendships. It's not that Jay is attracted to guys, he just isn't attracted to girls. Yes, his relationship with his military father was horrible…yes, he is very close to his mother. But does that mean he's gay? And who's he supposed to talk with about this stuff?

Jay is an avid Pittsburgh Steeler fan, second-string quarterback on his high school team, he loves the outdoors, and runs track. He's active in his church and is thinking seriously of becoming an Episcopal priest.

Yet he's getting nervous because his friends pressure him about getting a girlfriend and comment about his apparent lack of sexual desire. "What's the deal, Jay, are you gay?" they joke now and then. He's afraid to talk to anyone he knows, including his youth worker—because what if he is gay? Or what if he isn't gay, but the person he talks to tells everyone? No way can he talk to his parents about the issue—especially his redneck dad.

Finally Jay figures out a way to deal with his problem. He'll ask a girl out to the prom—there are lots of girls who have let him know they're waiting for his phone call—he'll pressure her for sex, the word will get out, and then the guys will leave him alone. He'll worry about his sexuality later.

1. What are Jay's options?

2. What would you do if you were Jay?

3. If Jay is a Christian, how could he consider the sex option?

4. Is Jay right in believing there is no one to talk to about this issue?

The Stats

About the relationship between self-esteem and coming out as a gay person to one's parents: among respondents 14 to 23 years old, young people with good self-esteem tended to be the ones who announced their sexual orientation to their parents.

Phillips Graduate Institute, 1996

By the Book...

For none of us lives to himself alone and none of us dies to himself alone. If we live, we live to the Lord; and if we die, we die to the Lord. So, whether we live or die, we belong to the Lord. For this very reason, Christ died and returned to life so that he might be the Lord of both the dead and the living. You, then, why do you judge your brother? Or why do you look down on your brother? For we will all stand before God's judgment seat. It is written: "As surely as I live," says the Lord, "every knee will bow before me; every tongue will confess to God." So then, each of us will give an account of himself to God.

Romans 14:7-12

THE ISLAND AFFAIR

Some stories ethicists have used for decades to capture the complexities of moral decision making. "The Island Affair" is one of those stories, and it has never lost its usefulness. This classic discussion starter forces groups of all ages to struggle with the difficulty of making decisions in real life. It may have been around for years, but "The Island Affair" is always fresh—because the issues that matter in life are always the same.

Let these circles represent two islands lying in shark-infested waters:

A shipwreck leaves only five survivors, who manage to reach the safety of one of the islands. Don is separated from his fiancee, Kenda, who is on the other island with her mother, Marge. Rick, a young man of about Don's age, ends up on Don's island. The fifth survivor is Winston—an older man, a loner, and situated on the same island with Kenda and Marge.

Two months have passed since the wreck, and the five marooned people have survived on what fruits and fresh water they can find on the islands. Don and Kenda are getting desperate—they are deeply in love, their wedding date is now only a month away, and they are separated yet within sight of each other. As each passing day makes rescue look less likely, Kenda becomes depressed.

While walking around her island one day, Kenda discovers a crude raft. It looks seaworthy—seaworthy enough, at least, to get her to Don's island. Suddenly Winston emerges from the underbrush. He has just finished making this raft. Kenda explains her longing to reach Don on the other island, and pleads with Winston to let her have the boat. Winston refuses, saying the raft was made for his escape, not hers. But Kenda pleads all the harder. So Winston makes her this proposal: if Kenda will make love to him, he will take her to the other island on his raft. Kenda asks for time to consider—then runs to find her mother.

Rescue looks hopeless, she explains to her mother—after all, it's been two months. And if she is to be stranded on an island for the rest of her life, she should at least be with the one she loves. Marge listens, then thinks quietly a few minutes before speaking.

"You sincerely love Don," her mother says, "and I understand your desire to be with him, but I am afraid the cost is a bit too high. My advice is to wait a bit longer. I'm sure a better solution will come and you will be glad you waited. But it is up to you to do what you want."

For several days Kenda considers her mother's advice. But when still no hint of rescue appears, she decides to accept Winston's offer. Afterwards, he in turn keeps his part of the bargain, rowing Kenda to Don's island. They embrace with delirious happiness, and during the day's conversation Kenda explains the bargain she struck with Winston, driven as she was by her desperate love for Don. She had sex with Winston, she confesses, but only because she loved Don so much. Yet Don is deeply hurt. He tries to understand, but despite his strong love for her, he just can't bring himself to stay with her knowing she had sex with another man. Kenda pleads with him to change his mind, but to no avail.

Meanwhile, Rick has been taking in this whole conversation from behind some bushes. When Don finally walks away from Kenda, Rick comes to her, confessing to have overheard everything—including that he thinks she is a very courageous and loving woman and what she did was admirable. He understands that what she did with Winston was the result of desperation and was really an act of love for Don. Rick tells Kenda that he would give anything to have a loving woman like her in his life. Kenda is deeply moved and heads off to the other side of the island with Rick.

1. Rank the characters from best to worst: Don, Kenda, Marge, Rick, Winston. Defend your ranking.

best _____

_____

_____

worst _____

2. Which person in the story is the most Christlike, in your opinion?

3. Was Kenda's sexual involvement with Winston defensible in any way?

4. If you were Kenda or Don, what would you have done?

MENTAL CRUELTY

Belinda's sister is ruining her life.

Belinda is 15. Teresa, 21, is severely mentally challenged. Because Belinda's parents both work, she has to care for Teresa every day after school (a hired nurse tends Teresa while Belinda is in school). Belinda knows she shouldn't feel resentment, but she does anyway. She wishes that either they'd hire a full-time nurse, or put Teresa in a home. Her parents say they don't have enough money for either.

Teresa often acts bizarre, embarrassing Belinda in front of her friends. Belinda can tell her friends don't want to come over anymore. She is so confused. Sometimes she gets angry at her friends because they don't know how to be kind to Teresa. At other times she is angry because she feels she's missing so much of the fun of her teenage years.

Belinda can't talk to her parents about the problem, but she knows that if she doesn't get help soon she's going to end up resenting Teresa—maybe even hating her.

"I sure am looking forward to the day when we can have genetically perfect babies, when no one has to have a mentally challenged child, when all kids will be good looking, strong, and without defect. When I see someone who is mentally challenged, I feel sorry for them. They should be put somewhere where professionals can take care of them. Think how much suffering would be alleviated if we could eliminate all the imperfect people".

Genetic scientist

By the Book...

The Lord said to Moses, "Say to Aaron: 'For the generations to come none of your descendants who has a defect may come near to offer the food of his God. No man who has any defect may come near...'"

Leviticus 21:16-18a

When they came to Jesus, they found the man from whom the demons had gone out, sitting at Jesus' feet, dressed and in his right mind; and they were afraid. Those who had seen it told the people how the demon-possessed man had been cured. Then all the people of the region of the Gerasenes asked Jesus to leave them, because they were overcome with fear. So he got into the boat and left.

Luke 8:35b-37

1. What are Belinda's options?

2. What advice would you give to Belinda?

3. Are Belinda's parents asking too much of her? What advice would you give to them?

4. How could a church youth group help Belinda on a daily basis?

The Stats

- ✪ Average teen's personal income: $3,692
- ✪ Teens aged 12 to 19 who get allowances: 29%
- ✪ Average weekly allowance for 13-to-15-year-old boys: $15.25
- ✪ Average weekly allowance for 13-to-15-year-old girls: $16.90
- ✪ Teens who work part- or full-time: 37%
- ✪ Average amount teens spend per week: $66

React
January 22-28, 1996

By the Book...

Children, obey your parents in the Lord, for this is right. "Honor your father and mother"—which is the first commandment with a promise—"that it may go well with you and that you may enjoy long life on the earth."
Ephesians 6:1-3

Fathers, do not exasperate your children.
Ephesians 6:4

PURSE-STRING PARENTS

She's 18 with only two months to go before graduation. And because of her 4.0 GPA, Debby has been accepted at a major four-year university in another state. In fact, she can hardly wait to leave home, thanks to her unbearably overprotective parents: 11 p.m. weekend curfews, no driver's license until she turned 18 (just two months ago), no steady boyfriends, and required church attendance on Sunday mornings, Sunday evenings, and Wednesday nights.

Debby's friends think she's crazy for putting up with such tight restrictions, but she's willing to wait until she's out of the house—even though it has been very difficult.

Part of the reason Debby has been patient with her parents' tight rein on her is that she understands why. Ten years ago her older sister, Denise, was killed in front of their house by a drunk driver. Her parents blamed themselves for not being careful enough, and they've never forgiven themselves. Debby's youth director at church has been more than a big help—she's been a good friend to Debby too, and encouraged her to be patient while she's still home.

That's why tonight was such a shock. Debby's parents announced that they had decided that it would be better for Debby if she did not go away to college. They want her to stay home and attend a local junior college instead. Debby sat there stunned as her parents explained the research they had done: the school she was planning on attending was in a dangerous part of town. In fact, a number of that college's female students had been attacked.

Debby surprised even herself. She stood up and slammed her glass down on the table. "I don't care if the school is in Bosnia!" she shouted. "I have been accepted, you were the ones who recommended it, and I'm going!"

Her parents sat silent for a moment before her father spoke. "I think you're forgetting one fairly important point, Debby. We are paying the bill for your college. The options are simple: you go to college here for the next two years and we will pay the bill, or you go somewhere else and pay the bill yourself. End of discussion."

1. What are Debby's options?

2. If you were Debby's youth worker, what advice would you give her now?

3. Has Debby already crossed over the line and violated the command, "Honor your father and mother"?

4. What would you do if you were Debby?

DISAPPOINTING PROMISES

Lanny has been dreaming about driving since he was in junior high school. His parents have told him that when he earns enough money to pay his auto insurance, they'll consider buying him a car. They didn't say exactly when they'd be able to buy it, but now that he's a junior with a job and an 18th birthday coming, he's sure it will be soon.

His 18th birthday party was uneventful—the usual array of presents— but as Lanny opens the last gift, he notices his dad signal to his mom with an anxious smile. Inside the box is a note telling him to look outside. The car! He just knows it's a car! Lanny rushes to the door, opens it, and streaks outside to see, parked in the driveway—

A 1974 Pontiac sedan. A four-door. Complete with dents and rust, Lanny notices immediately. He tries to act excited, but he hates the car. How could his parents be so clueless?

"It was your uncle Jack's," his dad tells him. "The engine's in great condition and it's very safe. It's not a great looking car, but it should get you through high school."

Lanny doesn't want to hurt his parents' feelings, but he never wants to be seen in that car.

1. What are Lanny's options?

2. Shouldn't Lanny be grateful?

3. What would you have done if you were Lanny?

4. If you are given a gift, are you obligated to keep it?

"You know what really ticks me off?

High school kids whose parents buy them a car or help them pay for it. Not only that, but a bunch of my friends expect a car—and a nice one, at that. I wish they'd spend a few minutes at my house. My mom works two jobs, along with me and my brother. All our money goes to one place—our family account. We don't expect anything from our mom, she expects something from us, and we gladly give it. She works hard to take care of us. Face it—most kids don't know how bad they have it. That's right, I said bad. They will never know how to appreciate anything."

Roberto, 17, junior

The Stats

Two-thirds of college students get money from home. And how do they spend the extra bucks?

- Food—78%
- Social activities—10%
- Transportation—7%
- Clothes—3%
- Cigarettes—1%
- Books—1%
- Personal items—1%

USA Today
September 23, 1996

By the Book...

But mark this: There will be terrible times in the last days. People will be lovers of themselves, lovers of money, boastful, proud, abusive, disobedient to their parents, ungrateful, unholy, without love, unforgiving, slanderous, without self-control, brutal, not lovers of the good, treacherous, rash, conceited, lovers of pleasure rather than lovers of God...Have nothing to do with them.

2 Timothy 3:1-5

"Here's what I believe.

You write a diary, you're an idiot. There is no way your parents aren't going to get nosy or accidently find it or look for it. They're human. If you keep a diary, then don't complain when it gets read."

Bernice, 19

The Stats

Students who have a happy family/home life:

◻ 1971—59%

◻ 1995—69%

Based on selected years from previous surveys by *Who's Who Among American High School Students*

By the Book...

Fathers, do not embitter your children, or they will become discouraged.

Colossians 3:21

There is nothing concealed that will not be disclosed, or hidden that will not be made known.

Matthew 10:26

The Diary

Mrs. Dawson found the diary accidently while she was cleaning her daughter Michelle's closet. She knew she shouldn't read it, but her curiosity got the best of her.

At first Mrs. Dawson thought it was the diary one of Michelle's friends...after all, these weren't the thoughts of her daughter...but no, it was Michelle's handwriting...yet it couldn't be her...

Michelle was a straight-A student, active in the youth group, a model child. Oh, there had been occasional arguments lately, but nothing serious. But the words Michelle's mom was reading in the diary! She didn't believe her daughter could say such horrible things about her and her husband. She had never heard Michelle use a swear word, but her diary was full of vile and outrageous language. There was so much...too much to take at one time. She had no idea her daughter had ever had anything to drink, let alone get drunk. The way she talked about boys, the sexual escapades she wrote about having with boys. It was horrible! The more she read, the more Mrs. Dawson got sick to her stomach. How could a parent be so wrong about her own child?

Later, Mrs. Dawson read excerpts of the diary to her husband. He was furious, all right—but not with his daughter. He was furious with his wife for reading the diary. But he too was bewildered. This couldn't be his little girl. This couldn't be happening. When Michelle came home that night she knew something very serious was going on. Her eyes full of tears, Mrs. Dawson held up the diary for her daughter to see.

"I hate you! "Michelle screamed at them. "I hate you! You had no right! You had no right!" She ran to her room, pulled some clothes from her closet, stuffed them in her backpack, and ran out the door shouting, "I hate you! I hate you!"

1. If Michelle were your friend and you noticed that she was acting totally out of character lately, what would you do?

2. If Michelle came to your house after leaving her parents, and asked if she could stay with you for a couple of nights without telling her parents, would you do it?

3. If you were concerned about Michelle, and her parents called you and asked for your help because you were such a good friend of hers, what would you say?

4. When someone you are close to starts making destructive decisions, what is your responsibility?

UNFAIR SISTER

It's tough when you're the first child. Especially if you're a girl. Your parents try to keep you from growing up for as long as they can.

Lauren can still remember every fight she ever had with her parents about growing up. A fight when she wanted to wear panty hose, a fight when she wanted to wear makeup, a fight over getting pierced ears, then a fight over the size of her earrings.

But now her younger sister Leslie is growing up, and she gets to do anything she wants. She's only 13, and already she has three earrings in each ear, wears all the makeup she wants to wear, and has a purple tint to her hair. It isn't fair, Lauren thinks. I couldn't even wear panty hose until I was in high school—and at 13 she's wearing lingerie-trimmed shorts, Victoria's Secret underwear, and silk pajama shorties.

Lauren has tried to talk to her parents several times, but they won't listen. They say that life is not fair, that it's a different world than when Lauren was a teenager. And besides, Lauren was the first kid—they now realize they were too strict. When Lauren counters with her frustration about not being allowed to get her driver's license until she had turned 18, her parents say that is a different issue. Lauren doesn't think so, and she's convinced her sister will be allowed to drive when she's 16.

Lauren wants out of the house. She's 18 and tired of being treated unfairly. She asks the parents of her best friend, Lisa, if she can live there until the summer. They say yes.

1. Do you feel more sympathy for Lauren or for her parents?

2. Do you agree that life is unfair? Should it be?

3. What would you do if you were Lauren's parents?

4. Do you agree with Lauren's decision to move out of the house?

5. Should Lisa's parents have said yes?

6. What options does Lauren actually have?

"Adolescents are the fairness monitors of the universe.

They spend hours making sure everyone in the family is treated the same. It's ridiculous. You cannot treat your children fairly, nor should you try. You learn as you go, as you raise each child, and you realize your mistakes and your successes. You change accordingly. Besides, each kid is different. What works with one doesn't work with the other. You can't be a good parent and be fair. Part of growing up is realizing that fairness is just a silly concept in a family."

A parent

By the Book...

Rebekah became pregnant. The babies jostled each other within her...When the time came for her to give birth, there were twin boys in her womb. The first to come out was red, and his whole body was like a hairy garment; so they named him Esau. After this, his brother came out, with his hand grasping Esau's heel; so he was named Jacob...The boys grew up, and Esau became a skillful hunter, a man of the open country, while Jacob was a quiet man, staying among the tents. Isaac, who had a taste for wild game, loved Esau, but Rebekah loved Jacob.

Genesis 25:21, 22, 24-28

OLD MAN, *Young Girl*

Melissa is a freshman at San Anselmo High School. She's 15 but looks much older. Melissa likes older guys—the younger ones, she says, "are too immature." Her mother has made it very clear that even though Melissa looks older, she isn't older—and therefore cannot date older guys.

This has never been a problem until now. Melissa, always active in her church, is now in the high school group. And she's become friends with one of the high school volunteer sponsors. A male sponsor. A 20-year-old male sponsor. Gordie is a total babe—and a strong Christian, active in his college's InterVarsity group, and just a great guy.

Melissa is not the type to sneak around. She honestly figures that since Gordie is a Christian, a sponsor of the youth group, and a nice guy, her mother will have no problem with Melissa and Gordie dating.

Wrong!

Her mom wigs out—not only forbidding Melissa and Gordie from dating, but going to the senior pastor of the church and demanding that Gordie be removed as a high school sponsor. The pastor complies. Melissa is furious that her mother would do such a thing. She immediately stops going to youth group and plans on secretly spending time with Gordie. By now, Gordie is so infatuated with Melissa that he's willing to continue the relationship as well.

Melissa comes to you, her best friend, for advice.

"Dear Diary,

Today was so great! Jason Ling wants to go steady. He is a totally buff guy—and a senior! I can't believe it. Any girl in school would die to go out with him. And he wants me!

It's going to take some real doing to pull this off. My parents don't know. If they did, they'd make us break up. Just because I'm a freshman, they think a senior guy is too old. Well, they're wrong. I'm not letting him go! My parents actually think every senior guy wants to rape every freshman girl. They are dead wrong. I've even talked to Jason about it, and he just laughs."

Darla

The Stats

Teen risk factors regarding sexual behavior:

- 53% have had sexual intercourse.
- 18% have had intercourse with four or more partners.
- 38% have had sexual intercourse in the last three months.
- 54% of sexually active teens used a condom the last time they had sex.
- 17% use birth-control pills while they are sexually active.

U.S. News and World Report
October 7, 1996

By the Book...

Flee the evil desires of youth, and pursue righteousness, faith, love and peace, along with those who call on the Lord out of a pure heart.

2 Timothy 2:22

Don't let anyone look down on you because you are young, but set an example for the believers in speech, in life, in love, in faith and in purity.

1 Timothy 4:12

1. What advice would you give to Melissa?

2. Do you think there's a problem with a high school freshman dating a 20-year-old? Why or why not?

3. Do you agree or disagree with the mother's response? If you disagree, what should she have done?

4. Do you agree with the pastor's decision?

5. If you were Gordie, what would you do?

Honor Thy Family?

The family of Luis has seen noticeable changes in his life since he, as they say, "became religious." He's stopped running around with the wrong crowd, his grades are beginning to improve, and his attitude around the house is better.

There's just one problem.

Luis's family is very close. They spend most evenings and every weekend together. But now that Luis is involved in church, he's gone all the time—Sunday morning and evening at church, Tuesday nights for his small group, and almost every weekend for some kind of youth group activity. When Luis is home, everyone else is on pins and needles, afraid to swear, smoke, or have a beer. They're all just waiting for him to say something about "living the Christian life."

So Luis's parents decide to have a heart-to-heart talk. They explain to Luis that they don't mind his new religion as long as he keeps it to himself, but they are concerned the family is being hurt by his absence from the home. Luis's brothers and sisters are complaining that they never see him, relatives are worried that he is not respecting the family—he is becoming too Anglo, they complain. His parents tell Luis to cut back on church activities—he can go to his small group on Tuesday nights and Sunday meetings, but no youth group activities on weekends.

Luis is crushed. He not only wants to be active in the youth group, but he knows it's the only way he can survive the streets. He's afraid that if he stops going to youth group, he'll be right back where he was a few months ago. He just can't believe his parents won't support him.

The next Tuesday night he brings this up in his small group.

1. What would you tell Luis he needs to do?

2. Is Luis becoming too Anglo?

3. Isn't Luis required by the Bible to do what his parents say?

"**My parents** are having a really difficult time with me because English is my first language, not my second. My parents were born in Mexico, but I wasn't. I am an American. I don't like the old ways of our culture, and I don't want to live by them. Mama and Papa just don't get it. They accuse me and my brothers of betraying our culture, of thinking we're too big or too good for the old ways. That is not true. They wanted to come to this country, they wanted us to grow up here, so here we are. We want to grow up like other kids, not like kids from the culture my parents left."

Carlos, 15

The Stats

How often do parents tell children they love them? One survey of parents with children under 18 found that these percentages of parents utter the three magic words at least once a day:

- 83% of all moms
- 71% of all dads
- 86% of all moms and dads between ages 18 to 34
- 75% of all moms and dads between ages 35 and 49

USA Today
February 14, 1997

By the Book...

Do not suppose that I have come to bring peace to the earth. I did not come to bring peace, but a sword. For I have come to turn "a man against his father, a daughter against her mother, a daughter-in-law against her mother-in-law—a man's enemies will be the members of his own household." Anyone who loves his father or mother more than me is not worthy of me.

Jesus, in Matthew 10:34-37a

The Stats

More than half of surveyed parents say the most important teen activity they monitor is the amount of time their kids spend with friends. Other teen activities parents watch (by percentage):

◻ TV—29%

◻ Movies/videos—11%

◻ Music—2%

◻ Computer use—1%

◻ Video games—1%

◻ Other—1%

USA Today
October 4-6, 1996

By the Book...

The Lord detests lying lips...
Proverbs 12:22

He committed no sin, and no deceit was found in his mouth.
1 Peter 2:22

The story of David and Bathsheba.
2 Samuel 11 and 12

Double-Date Trouble

Mike was tired of double dating. Why were Melinda's parents so strict? The Andersons felt that Melinda shouldn't date alone until she was 17. Mike thought that was ridiculous. It was hard to find a couple willing to tag along every time he and Melinda wanted to go somewhere.

One night Mike's friend Paul told him to tell Melinda's parents they'd be double dating with Paul and his girlfriend. Paul and JoAnne would show up at the Anderson home with Mike to pick up Melinda—and then, once out of sight of Melinda's parents, the two couples would go their separate ways. Nothing would go wrong, Paul said. What the Anderson's didn't know wouldn't hurt them.

Mike was persuaded—but he didn't tell Melinda until he was walking her to the car. She reacted, but calmed down after she said hello to Paul and JoAnne. It was all right to pretend that she and Mike were double dating, she reasoned, since she hadn't known about the arrangement beforehand. If something went wrong, it wouldn't be her fault. She decided to relax and enjoy the evening.

Later that night Mrs. Anderson phoned one of her friends ...who just happened to be Paul's mother. During the conversation Mrs. Anderson learned that Paul and JoAnne were right there at his house, watching television—not out on a double date with her daughter and Mike. When Mrs. Anderson hung up, she was fuming. Her daughter had lied. She had trusted Melinda, but never again.

When Melinda's dad heard Mike's car pull into the driveway, he walked outside, greeted them, and—though he knew the truth—asked how their date had been with Paul and JoAnne. Mike hesitated a moment, then said they'd all had a wonderful evening.

1. Rank the characters from best to worst: Mike, Melinda, Paul, Melinda's parents. Give your reasons for your choices.

best _____

_____

_____

worst _____

?

2. If parents give you unreasonable limits, do you have the right to go against them?

3. Does the Bible say that kids should do whatever their parents say?

4. If you were Melinda, what would you have said or done to convince your parents they were wrong about their double-dating rule?

Health Club Parents

A s far as Liz was concerned, her parents might as well send her to an adoption agency. They were never home. Both her dad and mom worked full time, then went straight to the health club for their daily workout. Many nights they wouldn't get home until 8 or 9, which meant Liz ate dinner by herself. And every other weekend (or so it seemed) they were gone running in some marathon or 10K or something. Liz wished her parents would think a little less about their bodies and a little more about her.

Sure, when the family was together, her friends told her how cool her parents were. Liz didn't think her parents were cool, but rather selfish, vain, and unloving. And although she had talked to them often about this, they laughed it away and told her that someday she'd understand what it meant to an adult to keep in shape.

Liz has another problem, too. When she's lonely, she eats. And just as her parents are obsessed with their bodies, so is she—Liz has been taking diuretics and has been vomiting to avoid gaining weight. So far her parents are clueless, but Liz is afraid she's started down a road from which there's no return.

1. What are Liz's options with her parents?

2. Is Liz's obsession about her body any worse than her parents' obsession about theirs? Why or why not?

3. What would you do if the Franks were your parents?

"I don't believe my mother. It's like she thinks she's 16 or something. Here I'm the one who needs more than the three outfits I have to make do with, and she comes home tonight wearing another brand new outfit—and it makes her look like a high school girl! She has the right to buy whatever clothes she wants, she says. Then she gets all emotional and says, What's wrong, don't I want her to look nice? She's a head case, I'm telling you. All I want is a mom that looks like a mom. I've tried talking to my dad about it. You know what he says? 'I like your mom to look young.' Sick."

Becky, 15, sophomore

About Becky's situation…
1. Do you see anything wrong with Becky's mom's taste in clothes?
2. Does Becky have a good point about her mom's style—or is it any of her business?

The Stats

A look at the proportion of kids who believe that certain adult behaviors are turn-offs:

- ✗ Chewing tobacco or snuff—98%
- ✗ Smoking cigars—92%
- ✗ Smoking cigarettes—89%
- ✗ Wearing black leather and chains—87%

Youthviews
February 1997

By the Book...

Therefore I tell you, do not worry about your life, what you will eat or drink; or about your body, what you will wear.
Matthew 6:25a

"Why is it that

when my parents are wrong they won't admit it? They pull rank or give that stupid parent answer, "Because..." or "I don't have to answer to you. You do what I say" or—and I just love this one—"We pay the bills around here, so we decide what's right and what isn't". I'm not asking them to be an equal, I just wish they'd admit their mistakes".

Jim, 17, junior

The Stats

"Clean up your room!" This directive, nearly half of all teenagers say, leads to the most frequent number of fights with parents. About one in five teens say room cleanliness is a less divisive topic, while a third say the subject rarely or never comes up.

Here are the remaining ire-raising subjects, listed in order of volatility and by the percentage of teens who say they argue often about it with their folks:

☐ School—35%

☐ Clothing/appearance—21%

☐ Friends—20%

☐ Music—19%

☐ Dating—16%

☐ Smoking—12%

☐ Drinking—10%

☐ Religion—9%

Youthviews
October, 1996

By the Book...

If someone strikes you on the right cheek, turn to him the other also.
Matthew 5:39b

Likewise the tongue is a small part of the body, but it makes great boasts. Consider what a great forest is set on fire by a small spark. The tongue also is a fire, a world of evil among the parts of the body. It corrupts the whole person, sets the whole course of his life on fire...
James 3:5-6

Wishy-Washy Parents

One evening a couple of your friends come by, and while you're talking you decide to go to a movie the next weekend. You ask your parents, and although they have never heard of the movie, they give their permission. The next Friday night your friends come to the house to pick you up and your folks ask where you're going. You remind them that they had given you permission to go to a movie.

"Oh, that's right," they say. "What movie was that again?"

When you tell him the name of the movie your dad responds, "Oh yeah...hmmm. I did some checking on that movie, and I meant to talk to you about it. Forgot you were going tonight. Anyway, from what my friends at work tell me, the movie's no good. You know, lot of explicit sex and everything. So I'm sorry, but I really don't think you can see it. You can go to another movie, though, if you want."

Your friends look at each other and grin. You can sense that they think your dad is a loser. And you hope they can't sense that you are embarrassed, humiliated, and angry.

1. Do parents have the right to change their minds after they've given their word to you, even if it's based on new information?

2. Was the dad unreasonable?

3. What would you have done if you had been this teenager?

4. What do you think of this teenager's reaction to the dad?

DECISION TIME

After a Friday night game at your school, a few of your friends invite you to go out drinking at a neighborhood park. You decide to go. After all, you figure, one beer isn't a big deal. Then an acquaintance of your parents drives by the park and sees you with a beer in your hand. You can't tell if she recognized you or if she saw the beer. But you are pretty sure that if she did, she'd phone your parents. As you're driving home from the park—having had only one beer—you can't decide if you should tell your parents you've been drinking, or wait and see if they confront you.

"Why do kids think drinking

is so cool? It is so stupid. Every party I go to, the guys who are drinking act like morons, getting in fights to prove how tough they are. And the girls who are drinking act like brainless, giggly pin-heads who think they're just the funniest people around. Honestly, they ought to look at a video of themselves. Drinking isn't a moral issue—it's for people with no brains."

Jake, 18, senior

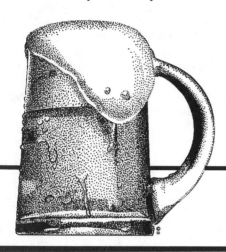

The Stats

44% of 12- and 13-year-olds know someone their age who's a drinker.
New York Times,
October 8, 1995

By the Book...

Who has complaints?…Who has blood-shot eyes? Those who linger over wine, who go to sample bowls of mixed wine. Do not gaze at wine when it is red, when it sparkles in the cup, when it goes down smoothly! In the end it bites like a snake and poisons like a viper.
Proverbs 23:29-32

1. What would you do if this were you?

2. Is having one beer the same as drinking a bunch of beers?

3. Is it being dishonest not to tell your parents about something they don't ask about?

4. Say your parents had no problem with you drinking one beer at a party. Would you agree or disagree with them?

The Stats

The number-one criterion among children for deciding what's true: personal experience.

New York Times
October 8, 1995

By the Book...

How long will you simple ones love your simple ways? How long will mockers delight in mockery and fools hate knowledge?

Proverbs 1:22

Be warned my son...Of making many books there is no end, and much study wearies the body.

Ecclesiastes 12:12

NO SCHOOL FOR THE MONEY

Pam took a deep breath. "I've decided to take two years off before I go to college," she said. Sitting on the couch, Dr. and Mrs. Holland said nothing. Pam knew it wouldn't go over well with her parents.

Finally Pam's father spoke, softly but firmly. "Pamela, taking two years off after high school is not an option. I don't know where such an idea came from, but you need to forget it."

"I can tell you exactly where I got the idea, Dad, if you'll listen."

Dr. Holland smiled. "I'm listening."

"It came from me," Pam said. "I'm just not ready to attend college. I don't know what I want to do, I don't really understand what I'm good at doing, so I'd rather take a break and not waste your money getting educated to do nothing."

Now it was her mother's turn. "Pamela, everyone feels that way when they start college. That is the purpose of an education—to find out what you want to do. You're just nervous and that's normal."

"No, Mom, I'm not nervous, I'm young. Too young. But there's more to this…I found out through the youth group about a two-year mission project in Africa. I've talked a lot to Pastor Doug about it, and he thinks it would be a great opportunity for me."

"You have been talking to your youth pastor about this?" exclaimed Pam's dad, now visibly perturbed. "What's going on here? Doug is supposed to help families, not make things worse. He should have talked to us about this before he filled your head with such impractical ideas."

"Doug didn't fill my head with anything except answers to my questions about where I might want to spend two years in a mission. I asked him. I brought it up."

"Pamela, I don't want to discuss this anymore. You will go to school next fall."

"Mom and Dad, you are not hearing me. I love you both. I am very appreciative of your support and direction, but I really feel like this is a call from God. I am not planning on being a missionary, I am not staying in Africa for the rest of my life. It's just that—well, because we have so much, I'm afraid I've lost touch with the poor of the world. I want to help them. I want to learn firsthand what matters in life and what doesn't. And I don't want to waste the money I will spend on school."

Dr. Holland stood up and looked at his daughter long and hard. "Pamela, there is nothing more to discuss."

Pam Holland went to Africa in the fall. Heartbroken, her father and mother threatened to withdraw any financial support for her schooling when she returned. The church board informed Doug, the youth pastor, that there was no longer sufficient money to fund the youth ministry of the church and that he was released from his job. Rumor had it that Dr. Holland, chairman of the church board, had engineered Doug's removal.

1. Do you agree with Pam or her parents? Why?

2. What do you think about taking two years off after high school?

3. Did Doug do anything wrong?

4. Was Pam wrong for going to Africa in the face of her parents' objections?

?

WEEKEND GUESTS

Your parents are gone for the weekend. They left you at home to watch the house. You're the only one there. Before they left, your parents told you that you could go out with your friends, but that you weren't to have anyone over to the house. A friend of yours is having a birthday the same weekend, and—despite your parents' instructions—you decide to have a small birthday party for him and a half-dozen friends.

Somehow, the word gets out at the football game about a party at your house with no parents. You try to discourage people from coming by assuring them there's no alcohol. No problem—the kids bring their own, and before you know what happened you have 60 or 70 kids at your house, stereo full blast, moving furniture so they can dance, kids outside getting into fights, and your mom's favorite vase smashed. Then a neighbor calls the police, who disperse the crowd—but not before they arrest several kids for underaged drinking.

You don't know what to do. The house is a shambles, everyone in the neighborhood knows about the party, the police, the arrests. What is so crazy is that you didn't want any of this to happen. You were just going to have a few friends over for pizza and videos. You know your parents won't believe you because you weren't supposed to have *any*one over for *any* reason.

1. What are your options?

?

2. What would you tell your parents?

3. How could you have kept kids from your home?

"I'm a cop. I just want to know why adolescents are so dumb. Why, when their parents aren't home, do they invite a bunch of kids over when they know the word will get out and uninvited guests will show up? This has been going on for years, yet kids still think they can have a party at their house without anyone except the friends they personally invited showing up. Go figure."

32-year-old police officer

The Stats

How much of their weekends do 9-to-16-year-olds usually spend with parents?

	Boys	Girls
All/majority of weekend	40%	50%
A few hours or none	24	12
Full day	19	22
Half day	18	17

USA Today
October 4, 1996

By the Book...

When an evil spirit comes out of a man, it goes through arid places seeking rest and does not find it. Then it says, "I will return to the house I left." When it arrives, it finds the house unoccupied, swept clean and put in order. Then it goes and takes with it seven other spirits more wicked than itself, and they go in and live there. And the final condition of that man is worse than the first. That is how it will be with this wicked generation.

Matthew 12:43-45

"Why do parents ground kids?"

It is so childish. By the time we get to junior high school, we're old enough to talk things through rather than have our parents confiscate whatever it is they've given us. Adults don't ground each other—why should they ground us?"

Larry, 14

The Stats

Percentage of parents who disciplined their children last year by—

◻ Shouting, yelling, or screaming: 85%

◻ Calling them degrading names (e.g., dumb or lazy): 17%

◻ Spanking buttocks with bare hand: 47%

◻ Hitting with belt, hairbrush, stick, or other hard object, on—

  ◻ The buttocks: 21%

  ◻ Other body parts: 4%

New York Times
December 7, 1995

By the Book...

Then the man and his wife heard the sound of the Lord God as he was walking in the garden in the cool of the day, and they hid from the Lord God among the trees of the garden. But the Lord God called to the man, "Where are you?"

He answered, "I heard you in the garden, and I was afraid because I was naked; so I hid."

And he said, "who told you that you were naked? Have you eaten from the tree that I commanded you not to eat from?"

The man said, "The woman you put here with me—she gave me some fruit from the tree, and I ate it."

Then the Lord God said to the woman, "What is this you have done?"

The woman said, "The serpent deceived me, and I ate."

Genesis 3:8-13

Grounded For No Reason

It's Greg's first night off restriction. Three months ago he did $1,100 worth of damage to his parents' car when he backed into a pole behind him that he didn't see. Two weeks earlier he had bumped hard into the curb, denting the rim of the front wheel. After the resulting flat tire and $75 worth of repairs, his parents made it very clear: one more accident and Greg won't drive for at least six months.

So tonight Greg drives very cautiously to the football game, to McDonald's, and then to the school dance. By the time he gets into the car after the dance, Greg is feeling more at ease with his driving. He turns the music up loud and heads for home.

He can't believe the red lights blinking behind him. He pulls over, hoping the policeman is simply trying to get around him. He's not. Greg was going 40 in a 25-mile-per-hour zone. The cop is courteous—but cites Greg for the violation, despite the boy's pleading for just a warning.

When Greg gets home, he explains to his parents that he was driving very carefully, that this is his first ticket, and that the speed limit where he was caught changes very quickly from 45 to 25.

Greg's parents are not sympathetic. They ground him for six months.

"Six months? You said if I was in another *accident*, I'd be grounded for six months—not if I got a ticket! This isn't fair! You're being totally too strict. It's my first ticket! You guys drive that fast all the time." As far as Greg was concerned, his parents were way out of line.

1. Were Greg's parents way out of line?

2. In your opinion, what was the problem in this family?

3. What suggestions would you give to Greg? To his parents?

Betraying Mom

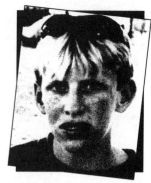

Ryan has dreaded this day ever since his parents divorced. He has lived with his mother since he was 11. He loves his mother and she is great to him, but he also loves his dad. Now that he's 15, he feels like he needs his father very much. His mother, who has never remarried, is still bitter about the divorce—which makes it difficult for Ryan to talk with her about his father.

Ryan gets along great with his dad and his dad's new wife. The last time he visited there, his father asked him if he'd be interested in living with him for a while. Would he ever! But his mother has made it clear that such a move would be a betrayal. Ryan doesn't want to hurt his mother, but he really wants to live with his dad for a while. He's suffered a lot of pain from the divorce, too. He doesn't know what to do.

1. What are Ryan's options?

2. Does Ryan have the right to live with his father for a while?

3. Whose feelings are more important—Ryan's or his mother's?

4. Doesn't Christianity make it clear that you are to give up what you want, to sacrifice your needs for others?

"I didn't get the divorce

—my parents did. My mom initiated the divorce. I have the right to live with who I want. I can't care about their tears. I'll live with who I want when I want. This whole mess is their fault."

Phil, 14

The Stats

☒ Proportion of American kids living without dads:

- ☐ 1960—8%
- ☐ 1970—11%
- ☐ 1980—18%
- ☐ 1990—21.6%
- ☐ 1993—23.3%

Youth Today
January/February 1996

☒ Since 1950 the number of American children living with only their mothers quadrupled from five million to nearly 20 million. Since 1970 the number of single parents has tripled.

New York Times
October 8, 1996

By the Book...

Honor your father and your mother, so that you may live long in the land the Lord your God is giving you.
Exodus 20:12

While Jesus was still talking to the crowd, his mother and brothers stood outside, wanting to speak to him. Someone told him, "Your mother and brothers are standing outside, wanting to speak to you." He replied to him, "Who is my mother, and who are my brothers?" Pointing to his disciples, he said, "Here are my mother and my brothers. For whoever does the will of my Father in heaven is my brother and sister and mother."
Matthew 12:46-50

DIVORCE SUCKS

The Stats

Teens from divorced homes in the '90s are less likely to get divorced than their counterparts two decades ago.

A UCLA study found that although teens who grow up in divorced homes will get divorced at a rate 27% higher than teens who grow up with parents who stayed together, that's better than the 139% divorce rate of teens who experienced family breakups in 1973.

Youthworker Update
October 1996

What Protestant and Catholic teens say about divorce...

¤ How easy is it to get a divorce?
  □ Too easy   78%
  □ Not easy enough   20%
  □ Don't know   3%

¤ Did divorced people work hard
   enough to save their marriages?
  □ Yes   71%
  □ No   29%

¤ Will they get divorced some day?
  □ Probably   36%
  □ Not likely   64%

KnightRidder Tribune
December 21, 1995

By the Book...

Jesus said to his disciples: "Things that cause people to sin are bound to come, but woe to that person through whom they come. It would be better for him to be thrown into the sea with a millstone tied around his neck than for him to cause one of these little ones to sin. So watch yourselves."

Luke 17:1-3

Carol was enjoying her new job as a youth worker. Except for today. One of the group's student leaders, Jodi, had been acting weird for the last couple of weeks, so Carol asked if anything was wrong. Now they're sitting in Carol's office after youth group, and Jodi is just plain angry.

"I can't believe it," she started. "My parents are getting a divorce! My mom says it's because Dad is working all the time and doesn't care about her. My dad won't talk to me about it, but he's told me many times before that Mom is always yelling at him, that he never seems to do anything right according to her, and he is sick of it. I don't care who is doing what. What about me?

"Why couldn't they have waited until I was out of high school? Why couldn't they have been adults and figured out a way to live together without screwing up my whole life? Sure, they've been unhappy and fighting for a long time, but so what? At least I was happy. Now we're all unhappy. Every day is another nightmare.

"Dad moved out yesterday. Today Mom went to a lawyer. Now I have to take care of her—she cries all the time. My dad is already trying to get me in the middle of it all—today he called and wanted to know who Mom's lawyer is.

"I'm getting angrier every day because my parents are so selfish they can't even think of their own child instead of themselves. Divorce sucks."

This is a tough one, thought Carol. I don't know what to say. I don't even know where to begin helping Jodi.

1. If you were in Jodi's situation, would you have her same feelings?

2. If you were Carol, what would you say?

3. Is Jodi correct? Are her parents being selfish?

4. What would you say to Jodi's parents?

5. If you were Jodi's friend, what would you do (not merely say) to help her?

STEPWITCH

Marci's stepmother was at it again. She was always yelling at Marci about something. "Clean up your room!...You have too much makeup on—get it off!...Turn the stereo down!...Your bathroom is a pig pen!" Marci couldn't understand what her father saw in this witch.

When Marci first asked if she could go live with her real mom, her dad was hurt and defensive.

"Look, Marci, Jan has treated you very well," he said. "You're free to visit your real mom any time you want—if she's sober and answering the door. All Jan is asking is that you clean up after yourself and abide by some rules. Any mother would expect the same thing.

"Marci, think about what you're asking. You're mother is not working. She is not sober. She can't take care of you. I know you love your mother, but you are being silly about this."

Okay, Marci thought, her mom is an alcoholic who gave her dad only temporary custody until she got her life together. But that was five years ago.

"Mom," Marci said next time she saw her, "I'd really like to live with you, but you keep drinking. When are you going to stop?"

"It is not easy being a single woman. Now you know why I divorced your father in the first place. He was always yelling at me about what he wanted."

"But, Mom, he wanted you to stop drinking."

"Sure," she said, "but why do you think I was drinking? He drove me to it!"

The discussion always went like this. Marci kept trying to explain to her mother that if she quit drinking, Marci would be there in a heartbeat. But her mom didn't get it—or wouldn't get it.

Marci decided to talk to her stepmother to see if she would be more reasonable. "More reasonable?" Jan responded, "Marci, I am not trying to make your life miserable. I love you as if you were my own daughter. I just expect you to live by the rules." So much for that, Marci thought.

Marci was waiting for her father after work. "Dad, I want to move in with Mom. I know she's still drinking, but I think I can help her. I just can't put up with your wife. She's a nice lady, I guess, but we just don't get along."

Her father sat down and was silent for a long time. "Marci," her finally said, "I can't do that. Your mother is an alcoholic. She has to get better on her own. She has to want to get better, and right now she doesn't want to. You are just going to have to learn to get along with Jan and stay right where you are."

Marci went to bed feeling depressed, trapped, and misunderstood. Then she remembered: I'm turning 18 next week, she thought. I can make my own decisions. I can do whatever I want!

"I know my stepfather is trying to
love me, but I don't want him to love me. It's my real dad I love, as screwed up as he is. I'm glad my stepfather makes my mother happy, and I'm glad he does-n't drink like my dad did, but I wish he'd quit trying to be the dad I never had. The dad I never had is still better than a dad I didn't ask for."

Marc, 15

The Stats

One of every six kids is a stepchild. One of every 11 adults is divorced—three times the 1970 ratio.

New York Times
October 8, 1995

By the Book...

The eye that mocks a father, that scorns obedience to a mother, will be pecked out by the ravens of the valley, will be eaten by the vultures.

Proverbs 30:17

---

1. Is Marci's stepmother unreasonable?

2. Why do you think Marci wants to move in with her mother?

3. Is it true that Marci can do whatever she wants at 18?

4. What advice would you give to Marci?

?

MACHO ABUSE

Your friend Jeremy is the son of an influential church family. He shows up one Sunday morning with a black eye. He shrugs it off, saying he got nailed in a neighborhood football game. No one thinks too much about it.

While playing basketball two weeks later, Jeremy takes off his shirt to be a "skin." You notice that his shoulder is a mass of dark purple bruises. After the game you drive Jeremy home and, strictly out of curiosity, ask him about his arm. Jeremy stumbles around for a second, starts to say something, then surprises you with the hostility of his response.

"It's none of your business! Forget it, will you?"

So you drop the subject, drop Jeremy off at home, and decide not to see him for a while.

It's a month later, and you offer to take Jeremy to a Young Life meeting. When you get out of the car, you hear yelling. You can't help but look through the big living room window as you approach the front door. You see Jeremy's father hit him.

You don't know what to do. You wait a moment before ringing the doorbell. Jeremy's father answers the door, acting as if nothing had happened. Jeremy comes out a few minutes later with a rising welt on the right side of his face. He rides to Young Life in stony silence.

"Girls get the sympathy

when it comes to abuse. I'm not talking about sexual abuse, but physical abuse. My dad has knocked me around for years. When I say abuse, I mean being hit with his fist, his foot, a stick, a broom handle, having my hair pulled, my head shoved into a wall. You'd think people would call that abuse, but not around my house. They all explain it away. It's an ethnic thing, they say. My mother, my family, even my brothers— who never experience my father's anger because they're not the oldest) consider me the problem.

I've just about given up. Pretty soon it's gonna be either run away or fight back. Believe me, I'm big enough now to lay my dad flat, but the family would disown me if I did that. So it looks like I wait until I'm 18. But I just don't know if I can wait that long.

Philippe, 16

The Stats

From 1985 to 1994, reported cases of child abuse increased 64%. More than three million cases were reported in 1993. Three children died each day in 1994 as a result of mistreatment.

New York Times
October 8, 1995

By the Book...

Fathers, do not embitter your children, or they will become discouraged.
Colossians 3:21

1. What are your options?

2. What could you say to Jeremy that would convince him you were safe to confide in?

3. If you were Jeremy, what would you do?

4. Is this abuse, or is it a very strict dad?

No Soap on Soaps

Mary Ann had her routine down. The VCR was set to record her favorite soap every day from 3 to 4 in the afternoon. When she got home after track practice, she'd grab some crackers and watch her favorite soap before her mom arrived from work.

But today the routine didn't work so well. Mary Ann's mother came home early, and there was her daughter, watching the soap. She blew up.

"I've told you again and again that I don't want you watching that trash, and you just ignore me. All they show is sex, sex, and more sex. None of them appears to work for a living, and they're all beautiful with perfect bodies and truckloads of makeup. Everyone's sleeping with everyone else. I am disconnecting the cable tomorrow and locking up the TV, period. End of story."

Mary Ann tried to reason with her. "Mom, it's just television. I know it isn't real. You watch those stupid talk shows about stuff like 'I married my girlfriend's dog!' What I'm watching is no worse than what you watch! Don't worry—I'm not going to watch a soap and then go and become a pervert!"

1. Do you agree with Mrs. Handley that soaps are bad?

2. Do you think Mrs. Handley overreacted?

3. What are Mary Ann's options?

4. What would you do if you were Mary Ann?

"I'm glad my family doesn't own a TV. We read at night, and I love books. I can't imagine what my life would be like without a good book to read. Yeah, I complained at first when we got rid of our TV—but now when I visit a friend, even though my parents say it's okay to watch television, I don't even want to. It's boring. "

Glenda, a home-schooled 16-year-old

The Stats

✪ Kids watch three to four hours of TV per day.

New York Times
October 8, 1995

✪ What motivates the average teenage character on TV?

  ✪ Peer relationships: 53%

  ✪ Sports/hobbies: 36%

  ✪ Romance: 27%

  ✪ Family relationships: 24%

  ✪ Society/community: 16%

  ✪ School-related issues: 15%

  ✪ Religion/spirituality: 1%

KnightRidder Tribune
August 17, 1996

By the Book...

Do not love the world or anything in the world. If anyone loves the world, the love of the Father is not in him. For everything in the world—the cravings of sinful man, the lust of his eyes and the boasting of what he has and does—comes not from the Father but from the world.
1 John 2:15-16

The eye is the lamp of the body. If your eyes are good, your whole body will be full of light. But if your eyes are bad, your whole body will be full of darkness. If then the light within you is darkness, how great is that darkness!
Matthew 6:22-23

SAYING GOODBYE TO CHURCH

Every Sunday for as long as Carol can remember, her parents have made her attend church. She hasn't been allowed to participate in anything that interferes with Sunday morning church service—no job, no school activities, no sports. In fact, her parents would travel with her to out-of-town volleyball tournaments just so they could bring her home in time for church on Sunday. Plus she's missed quite a few Sunday games.

But it's time to draw the line, she feels. Carol's three weeks away from turning 18—which will be old enough to make up her own mind, she tells herself. She just can't tolerate church anymore, although she believes in God. As far as Carol is concerned, church is boring and irrelevant. Even youth group is a drag—too many young kids. The only student in youth group who is Carol's age is forced to be there by her parents, too.

Carol decides to tell her parents of her decision the night before her 18th birthday. Her parents' reaction is, to put it mildly, heated. Before Carol can finish her speech, her parents interrupt her: as long as Carol lives in their house, they inform her, she will go to church. She can make her own decisions, they declare, when she is financially independent and moves out of the house.

"Forcing your children to go to church

guarantees that they will hate church when they get older. Parents should never make their children go to church. My parents made me go until I went to college. I haven't been to church since. No matter what age you are, church should be a place you want to attend. If you don't want to go, then don't go."

Megan, 19, college freshman

The Stats

▢ More than nine in 10 congregations admit to having problems keeping high school students involved in church, according to a survey of religious youth workers. On the other hand, only **8%** of the surveyed congregations say they have major difficulties keeping fifth and sixth graders involved. And it's only a minor challenge for just over half of the churches.

▢ Overall it appears that [quitting church] starts for teens between grades 10 and 12.

▢ About 46% said their congregations provide fair or poor budget support for youth programs, and 54% said their congregations show fair or poor support in general for youth ministry as a priority.

▢ The survey also showed that congregations with successful youth ministry programs focus on building caring relationships between adults and teens. Successful programs also offer opportunities for service and don't duck difficult questions teens raise.

The State, April 15, 1996

By the Book...

And let us consider how we may spur one another on toward love and good deeds. Let us not give up meeting together, as some are in the habit of doing, but let us encourage one another.

Hebrews 10:24-25

1. What are Carol's options?

2. What would you do if you were Carol?

3. Do you agree with Carol's parents?

4. Do you believe that when you turn 18 you should be able to do what you want?

UNFAIR AIDS

Garrett has heard about AIDS for years now, but he's never considered it a problem for him or his family. Garrett's mom and dad are active in church, public in their commitment to Christ, and happy in their marriage.

Now Garrett is sitting in his living room, but he feels like he is on another planet. His mother and father are telling him that they have AIDS. Years ago during a rocky time in their marriage, Garrett's father had been involved with a prostitute. She apparently passed the AIDS virus to him, and he to his wife.

Garrett's entire world crumbles in an instant, is ruined, devastated. Marital problems? Prostitute? How could God have let this happen? How could Garrett's dad do such a thing? Garrett worshiped his dad. How could Garrett show his face at school or church again? A more terrible thought: where will he go after his parents die?

Garrett bolts out of the house, running as hard as he can. His eyes fill with tears, and his emotions ricochet between anger and hurt.

1. What are Garrett's options?

2. If you were Garrett's friend and he showed up at your house that night, what would you do?

3. Should Garrett's parents have told him the truth about how they acquired the AIDS virus, or should they have made up something about a tainted blood transfusion in a hospital?

4. What would you do if you were Garrett?

"I can't believe

how freaked out everyone is over AIDS. It's real simple—you can't get AIDS unless you are a homosexual, do drugs, sleep around with a million different people, or get a bad blood transfusion. Well, I'm not homosexual, don't do drugs, and don't need a blood transfusion. I do sleep with girls, but they're high school girls, not prostitutes. Everyone acts like we could all get AIDS. I don't think so."

Darin

The Stats

AIDS is now the leading cause of death among 25-to-44-year-old males. It's also the fourth leading cause of death among women of the same age, reports the Centers for Disease Control and Prevention.

While AIDS cases appear to have plateaued among gay men, heterosexual transmission is still climbing. Now, in fact, AIDS rates in rural areas are rising faster than those in metropolitan areas.

Men's Health
July/August 1996

By the Book...

Do not be deceived: God cannot be mocked. A man reaps what he sows. The one who sows to please his sinful nature, from that nature will reap destruction; the one who sows to please the Spirit, from the Spirit will reap eternal life.

Galatians 6:7-8

For I am convinced that neither death nor life, neither angels nor demons, neither the present nor the future, nor any powers, neither height nor depth, nor anything else in all creation, will be able to separate us from the love of God that is in Christ Jesus our Lord.

Romans 8:38-39

"I'm tired of rah-rah youth meetings

filled with superficial, emotionally manipulative songs, humorous talks about the same old things—sex, parents, sharing our faith—and requests for decisions to do things we decide to do every week and end up never doing. Doesn't God speak to us alone, by ourselves? Why does youth group have to be so noisy, cluttered, busy, and chaotic? I'm beginning to think God isn't in the noise, but in the quiet. Trouble is, none of us kids are ever quiet."

Lance, 18, senior

By the Book...

The Lord is my shepherd, I shall not be in want. He makes me lie down in green pastures, he leads me beside quiet waters, he restores my soul.

Psalm 23:1-3

Everyone who drinks this water will be thirsty again, but whoever drinks the water I give him will never thirst. Indeed, the water I give him will become in him a spring of water welling up to eternal life.

John 4:13-14

Something's Missing

Alan attends one of the largest churches in Jacksonville, Florida. Youth group is an incredible place to be, filled with activities every day of the week—small groups, Bible studies, discipleship groups, service projects, mission trips. Alan is a very active member of the church. He's the senior class president, plays soccer, runs track, and takes AP courses. You could say that his life is one big activity.

Lately, though, Alan finds himself waking up in the middle of the night wondering who he is, where he's going. He never seems to have time to talk about the deep questions of his life, with his parents or anyone. (In fact, he seldom even sees his parents.) He can't remember the last time he spent a day doing nothing. Yet everyone around Alan thinks he's a great guy, a great leader with a deep and genuine faith.

But Alan is not who everyone thinks he is.

Lately he has felt depressed, lonely, longing for time alone. Although he knows a lot about the Bible, God, and the church, he feels detached from God, distant from Jesus. Something inside of him (is it his soul, he wonders) feels dry and empty. If he found someone to speak honestly to, he'd confess that he doesn't want to go to one more activity, one more service project, one more choir tour, one more mission trip.

What he longs to do is be close to Jesus, to feel God's presence—to spend an entire day alone, by a river, writing and praying to God. He begins to wonder if all his youth group activity is just another way of keeping away from God, of avoiding God. He wonders if God is trying to whisper something to him, but the busyness of his life drowns out God's voice.

Alan stops his youth director one evening and tells him about his longing for silence and solitude. His youth director listens patiently.

"Alan," he said when his student had finished confiding in him, "it sounds like you're just tired right now. You need to pray to God for more strength. Frankly, maybe you're doing too many things at school and not enough for God. If you stay active for God, he will energize you."

Alan drives home that night feeling uneasy about what he just heard. Contrary to his youth director's advice, he feels even more convinced that the problem is not the wrong kind of activity, but activity itself, period. He decides to call a monastery he has heard about a few miles away.

1. Is Alan too busy?

2. Do you agree with the youth minister's advice?

3. What advice would you have given Alan?

4. Have you ever had similar thoughts to Alan?

WHERE'S GOD?

This week at camp has been one of the best weeks of Janet's life. Although she resisted it at first, the campers have been required to spend one hour every day in a discipline of silence. Students were encouraged to journal whatever came to their minds. On the last day of camp Janet was sitting by the lake and reading over her journal entries. Her Wednesday entry was really bothering her:

> I have never felt so close to you, God, as I do today. I have never had this happen before. I was sitting here watching the sun sparkling off the water like a million diamonds when I was overcome with emotion. The tears surprised me as they overflowed from my eyes down my cheeks. I couldn't stop them. I didn't want to stop them. I just knew you were with me, and I could feel your arms around me, your love for me, your affection for me. It was as though you were trying to tell me that I was okay, that you were pleased I was your follower. I didn't hear any voices, I didn't see any visions, but this experience was the most real experience of God—or of anything—that I have ever known.

Janet was afraid as she thought about going home. Was God really present? Why had she never felt this before? Could this have been some kind of emotional experience and not God at all?

At the same time, something inside of Janet was tingling, something inside was telling her that she had just had a glimpse of God, and from that moment on she would never be the same. She also knew there was no way she could explain this experience to anyone, even her youth pastor.

1. Was this a purely emotional experience, or could this have been real?

2. Have you ever experienced God similarly?

3. How does God communicate to us?

4. Was Janet correct to not even try to explain her experience? Are some experiences simply impossible to describe or explain?

"Discipline of silence"?

Who came up with that idea? Our last camp we were forced to be silent for one hour. Why? I fell asleep. Doing nothing is so boring. I tried to get our camp director to change the schedule, or let those of us who were bored do something else. Could we at least sit around with some friends and talk quietly? Listen to music on our walkman? Nope. He was convinced silence was a good experience. This guy is from another planet as far as I am concerned. No more camps for me."

Kenny, 15, sophomore

The Stats

"There's a yearning on school campuses across the country for something different, a platform for [students] to be able to stand up and count for something. I'm hesitant to use the word 'revival' because I don't know if that's what we're in the middle of, but I do sense that God is doing a work in teen culture today in the midst of what looks like a very dark and bleak time."

That's how a Fellowship of Christian Athletes representative sees it.

Kalamazoo Gazette
March 16, 1996

By the Book...

The Lord said, "Go out and stand on the mountain in the presence of the Lord, for the Lord is about to pass by." Then a great and powerful wind tore the mountains apart and shattered the rocks before the Lord, but the Lord was not in the wind. After the wind there was an earthquake, but the Lord was not in the earthquake. After the earthquake came a fire, but the Lord was not in the fire. And after the fire came a gentle whisper. [In Hebrew, a "thin silence"].

1 Kings 19:11-13

"Praying is a waste of time.

Sure, some people seem to be miraculously healed, but it has nothing to do with God or prayer. It's just the luck of the draw. Read the newspapers—there are lots of people who have been healed who didn't believe in God or pray. If people want to believe that prayer helps, good for them. But it really doesn't help at all. "

Devon, agnostic

The Stats

Most Americans believe their faith helps in the healing process and that health officials should talk about this with their patients. In a survey for *USA Weekend* magazine—

- 79% said they believed faith can help people recovering from disease, injury, or illness. Of those, 56% said they have been helped by their faith.

- While 90% have never heard their doctor talk about faith, 63% thought it would be a positive step.

- Although some physicians feel there is a connection between good health and people's faith, other people feel those who embrace religion also make fewer unhealthy lifestyle choices.

**AP News Service
April 3, 1996**

By the Book...

"For my thoughts are not your thoughts, neither are your ways my ways," declares the Lord. "As the heavens are higher than the earth, so are my ways higher than your ways and my thoughts than your thoughts."

Isaiah 55:8-9

PRAYER'S DEAD-END

Just a few months ago Gary had felt so close to God. His small group had been praying for Mrs. Carrington, one of the youth sponsors who was having headaches and a loss of feeling in her hand. After a visit to her doctor, she was given the bad news. It was, more than likely, an inoperable brain tumor. It could be something else, he said, but both the MRI and the CAT scan were inconclusive. Whatever it was, it was inoperable.

Her husband refused to give up and found a specialist in San Francisco, where he took his wife for a second opinion. The doctor agreed that Mrs. Carrington probably had a tumor—but disagreed with the first doctor, believing that the tumor could be removed. Neural surgery was his specialty, and he was willing to attempt a new kind of surgery he was pioneering.

Everyone in the youth group—including Gary—prayed all day the day of surgery and were gathered together at the church that evening to wait for the results. At 7:30 the news came in—the doctors were able to locate the growth and remove it completely. The best news was that is was not cancer, but rather a cyst. Mrs. Carrington would completely recover.

Gary was ecstatic. He had never seen God answer prayer like this before.

A month later his father had the first of three heart attacks. The second came a few weeks later, and the last, fatal one, just last week. All during his dad's convalescence the small groups in the church had prayed for him. Remembering Mrs. Carrington, Gary was convinced that God would heal his father.

Gary sat staring at a picture of him and his father. He missed him terribly. How could God have let this happen? Why did God answer everyone else's prayers but not his? Mrs. Carrington was healed—wasn't Gary's dad good enough? Didn't they pray hard enough? Does God answer prayer, or is the whole thing a fraud? Gary just wasn't sure anymore.

1. If Gary had asked you why his father didn't live, what would you have said?

2. Why didn't God answer his prayer?

3. Do you believe God can heal?

4. What do you understand prayer to be?

FOREIGN LANGUAGE

Janie has been feeling like an outsider for about a month now. Ever since the youth group started having a monthly "night of silence," Janie doesn't understand what people are talking about. Last Sunday night the kids were talking about feeling "close to God," about "listening to God." But Janie doesn't get it. She's always thought she was a Christian—but this language is foreign to her. She's never felt particularly "close to God." What does that mean? How do you know it's God you feel close to? What does "close" feel like, anyway? And what's all this listening to God stuff? Does God speak in an audible voice? What are you listening for?

Janie makes an appointment with her youth worker to ask her these questions.

"I know this lady

who talks about God as though he speaks to her all day long. She says stuff like, 'God told me to open the door. God spoke to me and said I should call my friend. I heard God say he was pleased with me today.' Come on. This woman is wacko, right? People who hear voices are crazy. Nobody hears God speak."

Sue, 13, junior high school

By the Book...

The boy Samuel ministered before the Lord under Eli. One night Eli was lying down in his usual place. Samual was lying down in the temple of the Lord, where the ark of God was. Then the Lord called Samuel. Samuel answered, "Here I am." And he ran to Eli and said, "Here I am; you called me." But Eli said, "I did not call; go back and lie down." So he went and lay down. Again the Lord called, "Samuel!" And Samuel got up and went to Eli and said, "Here I am; you called me." "My son," Eli said, "I did not call; go back and lie down." The Lord called Samuel a third time, and Samuel got up and went to Eli and said, "Here I am; you called me." Then Eli realized that the Lord was calling the boy. So Eli told Samuel, "Go and lie down, and if he calls you, say, "Speak, Lord, for your servant is listening." So Samuel went and lay down in his place. The Lord came and stood there, calling as at the other times, "Samuel! Samuel!" Then Samuel said, "Speak, for your servant is listening." And the Lord said to Samuel: "See, I am about to do something in Israel that will make the ears of everyone who hears of it tingle."

1 Samuel 3:1-11

1. What does it mean to be "close to God"?

2. How do you "listen to God"?

3. How would you answer Janie's questions?

4. Is Janie an immature Christian because she doesn't understand this language of God?

Absent God

"It's a lot easier to believe in God

when a kid's parents have a happy marriage. Divorce is an ugly tearing apart, filled with lies and accusations that grind away the very foundations of adolescent life. Suddenly you can't trust your parents, you can't trust commitments, you are abandoned. Such struggles are difficult for adults, let alone children. It is amazing to me that a kid's faith survives divorce."

Adult counselor

The Stats

Of the general population, people with religious commitment are found to have much less psychological stress.

**Evangelical Press News Service
November 18, 1994**

By the Book...

My God, my God, why have you forsaken me? Why are you so far from saving me, so far from the words of my groaning? O my God, I cry out by day, but you do not answer, by night, and am not silent.

Psalm 22:1-2

At the sixth hour darkness came over the whole land until the ninth hour. And at the ninth hour Jesus cried out in a loud voice, "Eloi, Eloi, lama sabachthani?"—which means, "My God, my God, why have you forsaken me?"

Mark 15:33-34

Roger has always wondered why God seems so close when life is good, but so far away when life gets tough.. At church he often asked why it wasn't the other way: why isn't God close to us in suffering—when you really need him—and distant when life is going good?

Up until a week ago his questions were intellectual. Not anymore. His dad walked into his room six days ago at midnight to announce that his mom was moving out. She was in love with another man.

Roger's dad hasn't been to work since. He took an early vacation, and now just sits around the house crying. Roger himself is living in a daze. He thought he knew his mom, but he was obviously wrong. What was she thinking? How could she do this? That night he sat down at the kitchen table and started writing:

It's like someone put a block of ice in my heart. I still haven't cried, I haven't felt anger, haven't felt anything. I broke up with Amy. Stopped going to church. What's the point? I have tried to pray. I have asked God to make my mom come to her senses. Nothing. God's absence is so loud. He just disappeared. He's gone. It's like he never existed. I just try to get myself up every morning, make sure Dad is okay, get through school. I'm like a zombie. I don't think I care about anything anymore.

Would someone please tell me where God is?

1. What would you say to Roger?

2. Is God present when life is good and absent when life is bad? Would you rather have it—or has it been for you—the other way around?

3. Would you be concerned about Roger's behavior—that he broke up with his girlfriend and quit church, for example?

4. Where is God?

Unlikely Saint

Connor walked out of youth group, discouraged again.

This Christianity stuff isn't for me, he thought sadly. He just couldn't seem to do it right. Once again the speaker had told the youth group that if they weren't praying at least an hour a day, they weren't being good Christians.

And as usual, Connor interrupted the speaker with questions. "I'm thinking about God all the time—while I'm driving to school, sometimes during class, at night when I go to bed—but I'm not praying," he explained. "I'm just thinking. Isn't that prayer? Do I have to get on my knees and actually pray for an hour from some kind of list for it to count as prayer?"

The speaker answered Conner's question with something about prayer being a lot more than just a casual thought—that a person needed a definite time set aside to experience prayer the way prayer was intended to be.

Conner wasn't sure exactly what the speaker was getting at, but what he did understand just didn't work. For him, at least. Connor had tried setting aside a prayer time, but it never worked. His mind always wandered on about other things. Or he fell asleep. Believing in Christ was an important part of his life, but Conner figured he just wasn't the saintly type.

"I was shocked

to discover that most of the people we call saints were strange, odd, lonely eccentrics who were convinced they sinned too much. Most of them were haunted by a sense of their unworthiness. I thought people who were close to God *felt* close to God. "

Elisa, 16

The Stats

How often do Americans pray?

✗ 31% pray every day.

✗ 24% pray more than once a day.

✗ 16% pray several times a week.

✗ 10% pray several times a month.

✗ 9% pray several times a year.

✗ 9% never pray.

USA Today
February 9, 1997

By the Book...

Think of what you were when you were called. Not many of you were wise by human standards; not many were influential; not many were of noble birth. But God chose the foolish things of the world to shame the wise; God chose the weak things of the world to shame the strong.

1 Corinthians 1:26-27

1. Is thinking about God prayer?

2. Is setting aside a special time for praying better than simply praying whenever you remember to?

3. Do you think that anyone can pray for more than a few minutes without his mind wandering?

4. Is Connor correct about his conclusion that he's not the "saintly type"?

The Stats

Depression is the leading mental health problem in teenagers.

✪ Three to six million children under the age of 18 currently suffer from clinical depression.

✪ Thousands of others experience less serious depression, but no statistics exist since most cases go untreated and unreported.

Health—a Wellness Approach (1987); A Parents' Guide to Childhood and Adolescent Depression (1994)

By the Book...

They went to a place called Gethsemane, and Jesus said to his disciples, "Sit here while I pray." He took Peter, James and John along with him, and he began to be deeply distressed and troubled. "My soul is overwhelmed with sorrow to the point of death," he said to them. "Stay here and keep watch." Going a little farther, he fell to the ground and prayed that if possible the hour might pass from him. "Abba, father," he said, "everything is possible for you. Take this cup from me. Yet not what I will, but what you will." Then he returned to his disciples and found them sleeping. "Simon," he said to Peter, "are you asleep? Could you not keep watch for one hour?...The spirit is willing but the body is weak."

Mark 14:32-37, 38b

Wheelchair Questions

In her hospital bed Shauna lay motionless. She had never known the meaning of depression until now. Six weeks ago Shauna's life was like Disneyland. She had everything going for her—good looks, great mind, super family. She was a cheerleader, homecoming queen, going out with the captain of the football team, and already accepted at an Ivy League College.

Then her car was hit head-on, and she woke up paralyzed from the waist down. She'd never walk again, the doctors said.

During those first weeks in the hospital, Shauna was the most popular girl in town. Everyone came to visit her, talk with her, stay up with her, do therapy with her. The newspapers did articles about her, local TV stations interviewed her. Friends of hers came by everyday. Her boyfriend, Devon, brought flowers every day for the first week, promising Shauna with tears in his eyes that he would stick with her forever. Being paralyzed would make no difference to him, he said.

That was three months ago, and it had been weeks since Devon had dropped by. He had called once, though, a month earlier. Shauna heard he was dating someone.

Truth is, except for family, Shauna was alone—and probably would be for the rest of her life. Who wants to spend time with a cripple? Who wants to marry a cripple? Who wants to take a cripple anywhere? And where is God, anyway? The drunk who hit her wasn't even injured.

I've been going to church since I was two years old, Shauna thought. I've been baptized, born again—I worked on the last three mission trips. I read my Bible every day. I pray. So what happened, God? I guess it really doesn't matter that I believe in you—really doesn't matter that I gave up so much for you. I guess you don't exist after all.

And Shauna started crying, again.

1. It's easy to criticize Shauna's friends—but wouldn't most kids behave that way?

2. How do you feel about Devon—critical or sympathetic? Why?

3. If you had been in the room when Shauna went off against God, concluding that he doesn't exist, how would you have responded?

4. How would you answer Shauna's questions: "Who wants to spend time with a cripple? Who wants to marry a cripple? Who wants to take a cripple anywhere?"

God Fraud

A Christian since junior high, Carl was finally a senior. And although he'd been active in youth group for the last seven years, this year—what with his job stocking shelves at the grocery store, football practice in the fall, basketball practice during the winter, and track practice in the spring—well, he just hadn't made it to church very often his senior year.

And he discovered that, being away from the church, he was beginning to have serious doubts about Christianity. Until this year he had been so close to the church and the youth group, he didn't realize what others said about Christians. And though it wasn't flattering, Carl had to admit that much of what he was hearing was true.

Despite his off-and-on attendance to youth group, Carl's youth pastor still respected him enough to ask Carl to speak to the entire congregation on youth night. Carl made a quick decision: this was the moment to confront the other kids and the church with the truth. He didn't tell anyone what he was going to talk about until he got up that Sunday night and started speaking. This is what he said:

> Our church is one of the largest churches in town. It's the place to go. We have thousands of members and hundreds of kids in the youth group. Many of the kids go to my high school, and they're all popular. Our youth pastor is friendly, athletic, and a great speaker. We have the greatest programs and the greatest camps. We seem to have plenty of money in the youth budget, and we have regular mission projects as well. The adults in the church really support us.
>
> There's just one problem. It's all a fraud. Or worse, a joke. I'm not saying we're all phonies. We're just another social club. The kids in the youth group go to the same parties as everyone else. In fact, there isn't one difference between most of the kids in our church and the rest of the kids at school. The youth group kids have sex with their girlfriends and boyfriends, they make fun of people, they swear, they drink, they go to R movies or worse. They do what everyone else does—except they go to church.
>
> I'm not saying we're hypocrites. I'm just saying we don't see what the point is—we come to church and behave one way, and then go to school or work and behave another way. I think it's time for all of us to be honest. Christianity doesn't make any difference, so why even go to church? It's just another place to go. I don't go anymore. At least I feel more honest.

1. What do you think of Carl's speech? Do you agree or disagree?

2. What would you have said to Carl after his speech?

3. Do you think Carl should have said this in church without warning anyone?

4. Compare Carl's speech with some of the speeches Jesus gave to religious groups of people. What do you find?

?

"What bothers me

about Christians is they don't like the truth. They like to sweep it under the rug in the name of 'not offending a brother' or 'not creating dissension'. All they really want to do is avoid conflict. Yet I believe that conflict and confronting wrong is good. Christians are too nice for their own good."

Corey, 17

The Stats

Among Christians who classify themselves as born again:

- 39% believe "if people are generally good or do enough good things for others during their lives, they will go to heaven."

- 29% say there are some crimes, sins, or other things that God cannot forgive.

- 15% say the Bible isn't "totally accurate in all of its teachings."

Barna Research Group
March 18, 1996

By the Book...

When they heard this [Stephen's severe sermon], they were furious and gnashed their teeth at him. But Stephen, full of the Holy Spirit, looked up to heaven and saw the glory of God, and Jesus standing at the right hand of God. "Look," he said, "I see heaven open and the Son of Man standing at the right hand of God." At this they covered their ears and, yelling at the top of their voices, they all rushed at him, dragged him out of the city and began to stone him. Meanwhile, the witnesses laid their clothes at the feet of a young man named Saul.

While they were stoning him, Stephen prayed, "Lord Jesus, receive my spirit." Then he fell on his knees and cried out, "Lord, do not hold this sin against them." When he had said this, he fell asleep.

Acts 7:54-60

The Stats

A 17-year-old boy who killed a baby chicken to illustrate his pro-life sentiments for a debating class got more than a strong rebuttal.

He was slapped with a cruelty-to-animals charge. The Lancaster, California, student intended to demonstrate that if pro-choice folks find killing a baby chicken offensive, they should rethink their views on abortion as well.

The boy's supporters said his action was no different than those of hatcheries or slaughterhouses, and that it's a matter of free speech. But opponents don't agree. They claim the act is more severe because the boy purchased the chick at a pet shop and so it should have remained a pet—not a poultry item.

Youthworker Update
July 1996

By the Book...

Therefore confess your sins to each other and pray for each other so that you may be healed. The prayer of a righteous man is powerful and effective.

James 5:16

Jesus straightened up and asked her, "Woman, where are they? Has no one condemned you?"

"No one, sir," she said.

"Then neither do I condemn you," Jesus declared. "Go now and leave your life of sin."

John 8:10-11

The Secret Abortion

Fifteen months ago Denise had an abortion. It was an emotionally horrifying experience that took her nearly a year of counseling to get over. Now Denise feels that abortion is wrong. Yet she believes that God has forgiven her, and she's been trying to get on with her life.

For the past few months, Denise has been getting pretty serious with a new guy, Graham. He's great—one of those rare guys, she often thinks, who actually has standards. Denise and Graham have had wonderful talks, and among the subjects they've discussed is abortion. And, to Denise's private anguish, Graham has made it clear that he hates the very thought of abortion.

Yet the more serious she gets with Graham, the more she feels she must tell him what she's done. He might find out anyway—her old boyfriend and her best girlfriend know. Denise swore them to secrecy, but you never know. And if Graham found out from someone else...well, that could be a disaster. Denise comes to you for advice.

1. What are Denise's options?

2. What advice would you give Denise?

3. If you were Graham, and Denise told you about her abortion, what would you say? What would you do?

4. What do you think of Denise's opinion of Graham being "one of those rare guys who actually has standards"?

What Are Friends For?

Danielle and Natasha have been friends since grammar school. They and all who know them have been amazed at their close friendship. Natasha is liberal, Danielle is conservative. Natasha gets straight A's and plans to attend Stanford, Danielle does average work. Natasha's never been inside a church before, and Danielle is a committed Christian. Natasha likes to party on weekends, while Danielle attends church activities every weekend. When it comes to money, Natasha's parents are very wealthy. Danielle, on the other hand, lives with a single mom, and money's real tight.

Despite these differences their friendship is very important to both of them. There is nothing they don't know about each other and nothing they wouldn't do for each other.

Or so they thought until one day when Danielle opened the door to find Natasha there, obviously upset.

"Natasha! What's wrong?"

"We need to talk," Natasha whispered. "I...uh...have a problem, and I need your help."

"What do you need?" Danielle asked after they had retreated to the privacy of her bedroom and shut the door.

"I'm pregnant."

"Pregnant?"

Two hours of intense conversation followed. It was hard enough for Natasha to admit to Danielle that not only had she been sleeping with her boyfriend, but she had been involved with a much older college guy as well. Facing the painful process of finding out who the real father was, the trauma of the consequences of her duplicity, and facing her parents was more than she could survive. To Natasha, there was no way out except by abortion. Danielle believes abortion is wrong.

Natasha had already made an appointment at an out-of-town abortion clinic and wanted only one person to go with her.

"Danielle, you've been my friend for life," Natasha pleaded with her friend. "I'm safe with you. I need you to get me through this. Will you go with me? Will you please drive me? Please, Danielle, you're the only friend I have who I can trust in a situation like this."

"Good friends tell friends

when they're making mistakes. Good friends do not help each other make bad decisions, even if they disagree on whether a decision is good or bad. If my friend believes I'm making a bad decision, I should never ask her to violate her conviction, no matter what. Friends do not ask friends to go against their convictions.

School counselor

By the Book...

For we do not have a high priest who is unable to sympathize with our weaknesses.

Hebrews 4:15

Two are better than one, because they have a good return for their work: If one falls down, his friend can help him up. Though one may be overpowered, two can defend themselves. A cord of three strands is not quickly broken.

Ecclesiastes 4:9-10, 12

1. What are Danielle's options?

2. What would you do if you were Danielle?

3. Can it ever be right to help someone do something you believe is wrong?

4. If you agreed to help Natasha and she died of complications at the abortion clinic, would you be responsible for her death?

"Who's stealing

from whom? When you work for a big corporation and they deliberately limit your work hours to less than 30 a week so they don't have to pay benefits—that sounds like stealing to me. When a department store advertises a sale when the price is the regular price, is the store stealing? When gas companies falsely announce a shortage of oil and raise gasoline prices on gasoline, it looks like stealing. Insurance companies, corporations, oil companies are stealing from us. So when we take back what was ours in the first place, that isn't stealing."

Josh, high school graduate

The Stats

It appears that an increasing number of teens and young adults are ready and willing to lie, cheat, or steal to gain desired goals, according to a 1997 report by the Josephson Institute of Ethics. Among the findings:

▢ 37% of high schoolers stole from a store in the preceding year, up from 33% in 1993.

▢ About 65% of high schoolers cheated on an exam, up from 61% in 1993.

▢ 17% of college students stole in the past year, up from 15% in 1993.

▢ Nearly a quarter of college students say they'd lie to get or keep a job, compared to 21% in 1993.

USA Today
February 23 and 25, 1997

By the Book...

The commandments, "Do not commit adultery," "Do not murder," "Do not steal," "Do not covet," and whatever other commandment there may be, are summed up in this one rule: "Love your neighbor as yourself." Love does no harm to its neighbor. Therefore love is the fulfillment of the law.

Romans 13:9-10

STOLEN BARGAINS

Chuck didn't have the money, and it would be at least another six months before he could afford to buy a new stereo for his truck. Car stereos with all the amps Chuck wanted don't come cheap.

Now here he was at school, being offered the most amazing stereo system he'd ever seen—for $50. He couldn't believe it. In truth, he didn't believe it. He knew the sound system had to be stolen. Well, actually, he didn't know for sure, because he hadn't asked, and if he didn't ask then he didn't technically know it was stolen. What you don't know won't hurt you, Chuck thought. Besides, he couldn't go checking on every student at his high school. Hey, maybe the guy was rich, didn't need the money, and just wanted to get rid of it so he could get a new stereo system.

Chuck bought the stereo on the spot and installed it in his truck. It worked great. His parents were impressed that he was able to get such a good deal on the stereo. Chuck's new motto? "Ignorance is innocence."

?

1. Is ignorance really innocence?

2. What questions could Chuck have asked to find out if the sound system was stolen?

3. What if it was stolen and the guy lied and said it wasn't?

4. What if you had doubts about the truth of his answer?

5. To what extent is Chuck responsible to determine if the stereo system was stolen?

6. What would you have done in Chuck's situation?

YOU GOTTA DO WHAT YOU GOTTA DO

Today the coach will cut one more person from the basketball team—and it will be Ron, Chris, or Jim. All three of them have equal ability, but Ron and Chris have played basketball together all through junior high and high school. And now that they're seniors, they think they deserve to play together—and they've worked out a little scheme to ensure it will happen. Today during scrimmage they'll make Jim look as bad as they can without being too obvious.

During that afternoon's scrimmage, Ron sees that Jim is open—but passes instead to Chris. When either Ron or Chris do pass to Jim, they aim low or a little to the left or right to confuse him. Or they pass to Jim when he's not expecting a pass. In the final seconds of the scrimmage, Jim is open for an easy basket—but instead Ron drives towards the basket, passes to Chris at the last possible second, and Chris scores the winning basket. Ron and Chris are the standouts for the day. The next day Jim is cut.

Ron and Chris don't see anything wrong with what they did. Making the team was important. Jim had plenty of opportunities to make himself look good, and it's not Ron and Chris's fault if he didn't take advantage of them. Jim, a Christian, found out from a friend what Ron and Chris did. But what if anything should Jim do?

1. How would you describe Ron and Chris's conspiracy? Wrong or right? Smart or unsmart? Competitive? Normal? Unchristian? Simple survival?

2. What are Jim's options?

3. What about the Scripture that says, "If someone strikes you on the right cheek, turn to him the other also" (Matthew 5:39) or "I tell you, love your enemies" (Matthew 5:44)?

4. Do you agree with Ron and Chris that whatever Ron and Chris do, Jim has to make the team on his own?

5. What would you have done in Jim's situation?

The Stats

The following percentages of baby boomer teachers say their students have more of these traits in school than they did:

- Materialism—76%
- Anger—51%
- Competitiveness—48%
- Recklessness—41%

USA Today
February 4, 1997

By the Book...

In your anger do not sin: Do not let the sun go down while you are still angry, and do not give the devil a foothold.

Ephesians 4:26-27

"I work for this fast-food place. I make minimum wage. My boss treats me like dirt. I get the worst jobs and he's always yelling at me for every little mistake. If I need a day or a weekend off to do something with my family, he won't let me off. I mean, come on—I'm only in high school. It's not like flipping burgers is my life's work. The owner's a millionaire, while I'm just trying to earn some extra money. He's getting cheap help and he doesn't have to pay me benefits. So he shouldn't take advantage of me by acting like he's doing me a favor. I'm doing him a favor. I asked for this weekend off to go water skiing and my boss said no. So I quit. There are plenty of fast food restaurants looking for part-time help."

Ron, 16, sophomore

The Stats

Full time students who work—

☐ Less than 30 hours a week: 25%

☐ More than 30 hours a week: 31%

Part time students who work—

☐ Less than 30 hours a week: 16%

☐ More than 30 hours a week: 70%

USA Today
February 19, 1996

By the Book...

Better a little with righteousness than much gain with injustice.

Proverbs 16:8

Whoever can be trusted with very little can also be trusted with much, and whoever is dishonest with very little will also be dishonest with much. So if you have not been trustworthy in handling worldly wealth, who will trust you with true riches? And if you have not been trustworthy with someone else's property, who will give you property of your own?

Luke 16:10-12

MINIMUM WAGE REFUND

Greg has been earning minimum wage at a record store for a year now, working just part-time. He's tried to get a higher paying job, but there's just nothing out there. At first he thought he could make it on minimum wage, but the gas and insurance for his car are higher than he expected. He asked for a raise twice and was turned down both times.

He deserved a raise, Greg thought, since he was a hard worker, willing to help out when no one else would. But apparently that didn't matter. In fact, the manager let Greg know that if he wasn't happy he could quit, because he had plenty of people on a waiting list who wanted Greg's job.

So even though he had no extra spending money for things like CD's, having a job was better than not having one.

With the big July Fourth Holiday Sale coming up, the boss asked Greg to mark down prices on many of the older albums. Tom, a friend who also works at the store, let Greg in on a little scheme that worked last year for Tom: he had marked down—supposedly by mistake—some new CDs, arranged for a friend to buy them, then had bought them off his friend. It worked like a charm.

Greg decided there was nothing wrong with getting what you deserved. After all, the manager was cheating him out of money. This seemed like a fair way to get what he deserved in the first place—so he did it.

1. Did Greg deserve better pay?

2. Was Greg's manager wrong to refuse to give Greg a raise?

3. Was the scheme actually stealing?

4. Who was cheating whom?

Being a Good Witness

Thank goodness, thought Jeanne, that Brad was one of those youth workers who was always there when you needed him. He was driving her to the hospital to visit a youth group student because Jeanne was afraid to drive through downtown traffic, especially during the late afternoon commute.

As they pulled into the hospital parking garage, Brad cut too close to a parked car, clipping its right side, seriously gashing the door, and shattering the tail light.

Brad stopped immediately and told Jeanne to visit her friend while he took care of the problem, then meet her in the lobby later.

"Is everything okay?" Jeanne asked as they climbed back in the car an hour later to go home. "I feel kind of responsible...I mean, you wouldn't have been here if it wasn't for me."

"Don't worry," Brad assured her. "Everything's fine. It's not your fault."

Jeanne had almost forgotten about the accident when Brad called her a week later.

"Jeanne, I, um, have a little problem. You remember that accident I had at the hospital last week? Well, I decided not to leave a note—because the church hasn't been able to pay me the last few weeks, so I let my insurance lapse."

Yet someone had apparently seen Brad hit the other car and had called the police. The witness also wrote down Brad's license plate. Brad told the police that, yes, it was his car—but that Jeanne, not he, had been driving.

"Jeanne, if the church knew I was driving without insurance, I'd lose my job. Please do this for me: tell the police that you were driving, and I'll pay you or your parents back for the damage to the car. Besides, your parents have insurance on you. The insurance company will pay for it."

"But Brad," Jeanne protested, "you're asking me to lie for you and risk my own driving record, as well as my parent's anger. Isn't what you did considered a hit and run?"

"Don't worry about it, Jeanne. I told them we left a note and it must have blown away."

Jeanne was shocked. Her youth worker was lying...but she felt the whole incident was her fault...but lying for her youth worker just didn't seem right...but she'd feel terrible if Brad lost his job over this. It was Brad she had confided in when she had sex with her boyfriend. Brad had kept his word and told no one. So how could she now betray his confidence? She decided to tell the police she was driving.

"Everyone lies.

It's just part of being a teenager. If you can keep your folks happy by lying, why not? I don't think it's okay to lie all the time, and I don't think you should lie to your friends, but, hey, I'm sure my parents didn't tell their parents the truth either. It saves everyone a lot of pain. Lying is just the way to keep your parents from having a heart attack. Believe me, what they don't know won't hurt them."

Brenda, 17, junior

The Stats

Of Christians who classify themselves as born again, 26% don't believe they have a responsibility to share their faith with others.

Barna Research Group
March 18, 1996

By the Book...

Don't let anyone look down on you because you are young, but set an example for the believers in speech, in life, in love, in faith and in purity. Until I come, devote yourself to the public reading of Scripture, to preaching and to teaching...Be diligent in these matters; give yourself wholly to them, so that everyone may see your progress. Watch your life and doctrine closely. Persevere in them, because if you do, you will save both yourself and your hearers.

1 Timothy 4:12-13, 15-16

Not many of you should presume to be teachers, my brothers, because you know that we who teach will be judged more strictly.

James 3:1

1. What would you have done if you were Jeanne?

2. Did Jeanne owe Brad because he had kept a confidence of hers?

3. Does the fact that Brad is a liar disqualify him from ministry?

4. Was Jeanne responsible for Brad's accident?

?

JESUS THE CON MAN

It was in the beat-up garment district of Los Angeles's inner city that the youth group was spending a week with the Center for Student Missions. As Barbara walked down the street with her friends toward the Head Start Day Care Center, a homeless woman blocked her path.

"Could you give me money for food for my children?" the woman asked softly. "They haven't eaten all day."

Barbara felt something, like God was speaking through this woman—in fact, just like the Scripture they had studied in the morning in Matthew, where Jesus said that "whatever you did for one of the least of these brothers of mine, you did it for me." Barbara reached into her pocket and took out nine one-dollar bills and some change—all she had—and gave it to the woman.

The woman's eyes filled with tears. "Thank you, thank you," she muttered, then hurried away and disappeared around a corner.

"Do you know what you just did?" Barbara's friends asked. "She was just conning you for money to buy her booze. She sure made a sucker out of you."

Barbara wasn't so sure. She couldn't help feeling that God was present in the woman's eyes...or was it her imagination? When she retold her experience with the homeless woman at the debrief that evening, everyone agreed that giving that much money to people who will do whatever they can to survive was irresponsible.

Yet for reasons Barbara has never been able to understand, she has never wavered. As far as she is concerned, Jesus was present that day in the eyes of that woman. Barbara prays for her every day.

"Here's what I believe: when someone panhandles money from me, I give them whatever I have in my pocket. If they use the money to buy booze or cigarettes instead of food, that's their problem. I gave them the money to help them, and if they decide to use the money to destroy themselves, they're responsible, not me. My motives were pure."

Andy, 18

The Stats

Teens are less inclined to give to charity than they were at the beginning of the decade. But while the number of teens giving to charity has fallen, the money has increased. In 1991, the average contribution from a teenager was $56. In 1995, it rose to $82.

The Joplin Globe
December 11, 1996

By the Book...

"For I was hungry and you gave me something to eat, I was thirsty and you gave me something to drink, I was a stranger and you invited me in, I needed clothes and you clothed me, I was sick and you looked after me, I was in prison and you came to visit me."

Then the righteous will answer him, "Lord, when did we see you hungry and feed you, or thirsty and give you something to drink? When did we see you a stranger and invite you in, or needing clothes and clothe you? When did we see you sick or in prison and go to visit you?"

The King will reply, "I tell you the truth, whatever you did for one of the least of these brothers of mine, you did for me."

Matthew 25:35-40

1. Was Barbara irresponsible?

2. Have you ever had an experience like Barbara's? What did you do?

3. Did Barbara really see Jesus in the poor, or was she conned?

POVERTY IS HORRIBLE...
FOR A LITTLE WHILE

The baby died in her arms.

Lisa had taken a trip to Haiti with her youth group. The 17-year-old was in the middle of a two-week mission trip to help the poor when, during the building of a home for a family, their baby died. Lisa had heard about starving children, but never had she imagined that starvation could be so terrible. Having never been hungry in her life, having never known anyone who was hungry, she felt guilty, selfish, sick to her stomach, and angry. Guilty because she had so much and had never helped anyone in need before. Angry because it wasn't fair for these people to have so little when Americans had so much.

With the lifeless baby in her arms, Lisa vowed to dedicate her life to relieving hunger wherever she could. Tears filled her eyes. She wanted to go home and scream to everyone how selfish they were. But now all she could do was cry.

It was a sad funeral, with only the youth group and the family present. The body of the infant was buried in a shallow grave. Lisa returned home determined to make a difference.

Three months later Lisa was Christmas shopping in a mall when she saw a young Haitian mother with her baby. She remembered the baby she had held during the summer—the baby who died. She remembered the emotional commitment she had made to help the poor—and she realized how quickly she had forgotten that commitment. Lisa had tried so hard when she came home…though everyone was sympathetic, nothing had changed. There was the annual family vacation, cheerleading camp, school shopping, and now it was three months later. Lisa wanted to do something, but what? Maybe next year she would go on the trip to Haiti again, if she didn't have a job.

1. Does Lisa have anything to feel guilty about?

2. Are you sympathetic or critical of Lisa?

3. Have you ever been emotionally moved by poverty or extreme need —and later forgotten about it?

4. What was Lisa's responsibility after this experience? What should she have done?

"High school kids are so phony.

You go to a class or conference on racism or hunger, and kids sit around crying and saying how concerned they are. Then when class is over, you see the same kids making fun of some other kid and talking about all the stuff they "need." Oh, and the environment—yeah, they're big on recycling …then they throw their trash wherever they feel like it. You should see our school. Kids say they're not going to be like their parents. But they already are. This generation is basically a bunch of spoiled, selfish, self-centered brats. We pretend to care about the world, but we really don't care about anything except money, clothes, friends, sex, music, and having a good time."

Claudia, 18, senior

The Stats

Children made up nearly half (48%) of the chronically poor in 1992 and 1993, living in families that stayed below the poverty line in every month of those years, the Census Bureau reported. And more than 8% of all American children were chronically poor during that time period.

Youthworker Update
October 1996

By the Book...

Do not merely listen to the word, and so deceive yourselves. Do what it says. Anyone who listens to the word but does not do what it says is like a man who looks at his face in a mirror and, after looking at himself, goes away and immediately forgets what he looks like.
James 1:22-24

"I learned something

on this mission trip. I am a very selfish person. I went to Jamaica to help the poor, and I ended up being helped. It took so little to make them happy. They weren't afraid to work—in fact, they worked circles around us. Though they had very little, they always gave to others. Maybe it's us Americans who think we have so much who are really the poor ones. Poverty is cruel and ugly, but wealth has its ugliness, too."

Melinda, 14

The Stats

In 1991 half of all American 12-to-17-year-olds gave to charity. In 1995 only 41% of them gave, according to a Gallup survey of 800 foundations and corporate giving programs.

The Joplin Globe
December 11, 1996

By the Book...

Woe to you, teachers of the law and Pharisees, you hypocrites! You travel over land and sea to win a single convert, and when he becomes one, you make him twice as much a son of hell as you are.

Matthew 23:15

"I was hungry and you gave me nothing to eat, I was thirsty and you gave me nothing to drink, I was a stranger and you did not invite me in, I needed clothes and you did not clothe me, I was sick and in prison and you did not look after me." They will also answer, "Lord, when did we see you hungry or thirsty or a stranger or needing clothes or sick or in prison, and did not help you?" He will reply, "I tell you the truth, whatever you did not do for one of the least of these, you did not do for me."

Matthew 25:42-45

Ministering to the Poor
...WHAT A BORE

With $30,000 in the bank that they had raised during the previous year, the youth group was making its final plans to travel to Mexico and build 10 houses for the poor. But Melanie and James wouldn't have any part of it. Why spend $30,000 to build houses for people in a foreign country, they said, when our own country has thousands, hundreds of thousands of homeless? We should take care of our people first before we take care of other people.

The other kids in the youth group didn't like what Melanie and James were saying. First of all, if you build a house in America, you have to build it to code. Building a house in Mexico is more like building a garage—no electricity, no water, but it's still warm, dry, adequate shelter from rain and cold. Besides, to build a home in the U.S. would cost 15 to 30 times as much as it would in Mexico.

In fact, the whole youth group was angry with Melanie and James for causing this split among them. The two teenagers were even dividing the adults in the church, and the other kids feared that if this kept up, soon nothing would be built and nobody would be helped. Besides, if Melanie and James were so concerned about the homeless in the U.S., then why weren't they helping them? They weren't doing anything for the homeless except arguing that they should be helped instead of Mexican families. The entire church was polarized over the issue.

After a lengthy meeting, the church board decided to cancel the Mexico trip, to have no project this year, and instead take the year to find a project that could involve everyone. During the next several months 15 families left the church over the issue, Melanie and James moved out of town, and when it came time a year later to do a summer project, it never happened.

1. Do you agree with James and Melanie that we should help the poor in our country before we help the poor in other countries?

2. Who is mostly to blame for the cancellation of the project and for two years of no service project?

3. If you were on the church board, what solution would you have suggested?

RACISM REALITY CHECK

First Church sends a youth servant team out every summer. In three months they usually cover hundreds of miles and work in many small towns in the southern states around them. This summer they've decided to help rebuild three black churches that were burned down. In cooperation with a number of denominational groups, they believe they can make a substantial contribution to the three churches. Everyone is excited about this year's summer mission.

And then Lisa comes home from college to work with the youth team—and she brings her black boyfriend with her. Even though First Church is in the deep South, Lisa thinks her church is beyond racism. She quickly learns how wrong she is.

Kids in the youth group stare, act funny, distant, even cool to both Lisa and Carver. Yet what's even more difficult for Lisa to understand is the response of the adult leaders—the men and women of God whom Lisa has admired while growing up in the church. These are the same adults who taught her the meaning of the Christian faith, of love—of unconditional love. Yet now they are noticeably shaken and uneasy about Lisa and Carver.

Talking informally with the youth group, these adults make it clear that they are not racists, but realists. "You can't go into the deep South and help people," they reason, "if you flaunt your interracial relationship in front of them."

Nevertheless, the couple joins the team. When they arrive at their first church to begin working, blacks and whites together, it's clear that neither the black nor the white kids they work with on the team are comfortable with Lisa and Carver's relationship. Lisa is shocked. How can the church condone racism, she thought? How can the very community of blacks and whites who are working together to rebuild a black church have trouble with a black and a white relationship? It was crazy.

To Lisa and Carver their relationship is a powerful testimony to the fact that all are one in Christ. There is no racism in Jesus. But as the summer progresses, tensions get worse by the day. Resentment builds when some members of the group mention that maybe Lisa and Carver's relationship is hindering the group's ministry in the small towns. They feel that interracial relationships are becoming more of an issue than Jesus.

Finally three team members approach Lisa and Carver late one night. Something has to be done, they say, to restore unity in the servant group and to alleviate the tension in the small towns where they minister.

"Christians like to help black people—they just don't like to work with them, date them, be friends with them, live in the same neighborhood as them, go to church with them, socialize with them, or have anything to do with them. Helping black people becomes just another form of racism.

16-year-old black sophomore female

The Stats

Seventy-one percent of 9-to-13-year-olds said they have close friends of a different race or ethnic origin.

New York Times
October 8, 1995

By the Book...

Be careful, however, that the exercise of your freedom does not become a stumbling block to the weak...So this weak brother, for whom Christ died, is destroyed by your knowledge...Therefore, if what I eat causes my brother to fall into sin, I will never eat meat again, so that I will not cause him to fall.

1 Corinthians 8: 9,11,13

All chapters...

Book of Ruth

There is neither Jew nor Greek, slave nor free, male nor female, for you are all one in Christ Jesus.

Galatians 3:28

?

1. If you were Lisa or Carver, what would you say to the team?

2. Is it right to force a group of racists to accept your point of view when you are trying to help them?

3. What are Lisa and Carver's options at this point?

4. How do you respond to the statement, "We're not racists, we're realists"?

"Anyone who denies being a racist is a liar.

Racism is part of our humanity. We can't deny it, but we can control it. Racism doesn't mean we put others down—it just means we prefer people who are like us. Nothing wrong with that. Blacks are just as racist as whites. Jews are racist against Palestinians. White liberals are such hypocrites. Racism is actually good for people, because it purifies the races—all races.

Stan, white 19-year-old skinhead

The Stats

Here's what high achieving teens say are the results of affirmative action and pro-immigration policies:

◻ It will be harder to get the job I want: 59%

◻ It will be harder to get into the college I want: 49%

◻ Society is more interesting: 39%

◻ Society is more dangerous: 29%

◻ There's too many languages spoken in the U.S.: 29%

◻ Schools aren't as good: 22%

◻ Schools are better: 9%

San Antonio Express News
November 19, 1996

By the Book...

But you are a chosen people, a royal priesthood, a holy nation, a people belonging to God, that you may declare the praises of him who called you out of darkness into his wonderful light. Once you were not a people, but now you are the people of God; once you had not received mercy, but now you have received mercy.

1 Peter 2:9-10

Daughter Makes the Difference

Mr. Tallerico, the head of the Vestry at St. John's Church, has been a strong voice for keeping the church downtown—despite the changing racial make-up of the area. Most of their neighboring downtown churches have moved to the suburbs, but Mr. Tallerico has been a staunch believer that the church is made from all races. "There is no room for racism in the body of Christ," he would often say. Sophia Tallerico is proud of her father's stance and has always fought racism herself wherever she's seen it.

She was so glad to come home at Thanksgiving during her freshman year at college because she had an announcement to make.

"Daddy," she said, "I've met The One." She and her father had joked for many years about how God picks The One. "His name is Carlos and he's from the Dominican Republic. Look at his picture."

Mr. Tallerico did—and Sophia could see immediately that he was not pleased.

"From the Dominican Republic?" he asked warily.

"Yes, Dad."

"He looks like he's from Harlem."

Sophia couldn't believe what she was hearing. "You mean because he's black?"

"Yes," said Mr. Tallerico, "he is black."

"Dad, he's Dominican. But why should you, of all people, care if he's black or brown or white?"

"It makes a lot of difference, Sugar. Your cultures, your backgrounds are so different. Think of your children and the reaction of people aro—"

"It's because he's black, isn't it?" Sophia couldn't hold back any longer. "You don't want your daughter involved with a black man. I can't believe this. My father, the crusader to keep the church integrated, doesn't want his own family integrated!"

"Sophia!" Mr. Tallerico's voice was tense with anger. "It's one thing to have black people in your church. It's quite another to have them in your family. That should be obvious. We are completely different cultures! Can't you see the difference?"

She eventually broke up with The One—and became very distant from her father, whom she hasn't spoken to for three years.

1. Was Mr. Tallerico a racist?

2. Can someone accept something in one setting, yet reject that same thing in another setting?

3. How would your parents respond if you became serious with someone with a different ethnic background?

4. Why do you think Sophia cut herself off from her father? Was it understandable? Was it right? What else could she have done?

DYING IS NOT FUN

Leukemia.

Klarissa will never forget the day her doctor spoke that word. She hadn't been feeling well—tired, joints painful, ankles swollen—but everyone had the flu that year. Except Klarissa.

There they were, her mother and stepdad, sitting in the silent aftermath of the word, the horrible word. Everyone cried that day in the doctor's office—everyone but Klarissa. She couldn't cry. She couldn't be sad. But she was angry. Angry with God, angry with the doctor, angry with everything. Leukemia wasn't fair, it wasn't good, it wasn't right. All these years Klarissa sat in youth group, went to camp, talked about Jesus and how much she loved him and he loved her. Now it all seemed like empty, cruel gibberish. If there is a God, she decided, he doesn't demonstrate his love for someone by giving them leukemia.

But the anger was nothing compared to the loneliness Klarissa experienced. When she used to feel lonely before, it wasn't anything like this. When her youth director led discussions about loneliness, the group didn't know what they were talking about. They weren't talking about loneliness, Klarissa thought—they were talking about the silly adolescent experience of feeling like people didn't like you.

But loneliness—real, anguishing loneliness—was what Klarissa experienced now. She could feel her friends treating her differently—the patronizing, gosh-we-feel-sorry-for-you-it-must-be-awful-I'm-glad-it-isn't-me attitude all her friends now had. Even her parents, her brother, her uncles and aunts—even in their words Klarissa could hear their relief it wasn't them. Sure, everyone's words were loving, kind, compassionate—but it was a thin veneer over their own fear of death. Klarissa was a marked girl. She knew it, her friends knew it, the doctors knew it. It was the absolute terror of being alone, not the leukemia, that was killing Klarissa.

From the day Klarissa heard the word leukemia in the doctor's office, she stopped going to church. She never mentioned the name of Jesus except in bitterness. She remained friends with kids from the youth group and she appreciated their prayers for her, but Klarissa figured that from then on, she was on her own. Jesus and God are great when you're in good health or when you're old, she concluded, but not when your whole life is being robbed from you by the very one who supposedly gives you life. Klarissa made up her mind that if she was to beat death, it'd be because of her determination, not because of some sort of supposed "love" of Jesus—unless, of course, this Jesus she used to believe in showed up pretty soon. And that didn't seem very likely.

"My little sister

was diagnosed with cancer. After the surgery, we had to take her to Children's Hospital every Thursday for her meds, for chemotherapy. Every day I prayed for her healing. Then one day I had to stand with my sister in line with 10 other little boys and girls who had cancer as well. It was then I realized I couldn't pray for Zoe's healing again. How could I ask God to heal Zoe and not heal all the other children? Surely, God doesn't heal only the children of those who pray, does he? He doesn't answer only Christians' prayers, right? After that I never prayed again for her healing."

Wil, 22, college senior

By the Book...

For to me, to live is Christ and to die is gain.

Philippians 1:21

What a wretched man I am! Who will rescue me from this body of death?

Romans 7:24

Could you not keep watch for one hour?

Mark 14:37

1. Can you blame Klarissa for feeling the way she did about Jesus?

2. What would you say to or do for Klarissa in an attempt to change her mind?

3. How could the youth group communicate to Klarissa the reality and presence of Jesus?

4. What do you think about Klarissa's terror of being alone? Have you ever experienced this kind of loneliness?

ALANA'S MYSTERY

By the Book...

Now we see but a poor reflection; then we shall see face to face. Now I know in part; then I shall know fully, even as I am fully known.

1 Corinthians 13:12

Then I saw a new heaven and a new earth, for the first heaven and the first earth had passed away, and there was no longer any sea. I saw the Holy City, the new Jerusalem, coming down out of heaven from God, prepared as a bride beautifully dressed for her husband. And I heard a loud voice from the throne saying, "Now the dwelling of God is with men, and he will live with them. They will be his people, and God himself will be with them and be their God. He will wipe every tear from their eyes. There will be no more death or mourning or crying or pain, for the old order of things has passed away."

Revelation 21:1-4

A nybody in Jacksonville knew that Alana was an incredible girl, Rob thought. Here she was, her senior year—valedictorian, homecoming queen, president of the district youth council at church, member of the award-winning school madrigal choir, cheerleader, and one of the top distance runners in the state. Her faith was vibrant, active, and courageous. Alana spearheaded the "See You at the Pole" day at her school and actively talked about her faith every opportunity she had. And she left no doubt in anyone's mind that it was God who made all her accomplishments possible.

Rob believed her. He and Alana had been dating their entire senior year, and she was truly the most amazing girl he had ever met. Never mind that Alana was black, that she had never known her father, that she had grown up with a single mom who raised Alana and four other children by working two jobs. Never mind that when her mom died, Alana and her brothers and sisters were placed in foster homes. Alana had a picture of her mother on her desk and every day before she did anything else she'd kiss the picture of her mother. "For you and Jesus, Mom," she say. God had great things ahead for Alana.

Two weeks before graduation on a bright, sunny afternoon, Rob and Alana were out shopping for a graduation dress. Rob was turning left at a green light into the shopping center when he saw a red blur outside the passenger window. That was the last thing he remembered until he woke up in the hospital. A drunk driver had gone through the red light and slammed into the passenger door of Rob's car at 60 miles an hour. Rob had a slight concussion and a broken left arm. But Alana, Rob thought fuzzily...what happened to Alana?

There were 2,000 stunned people at Alana's funeral. The entire high school must have been there, plus every member from her church. Although everyone tried to make this a celebration of Alana's life and hope in God, no amount of ceremony could drown out the question in everyone's mind: "Why?" This was such a waste. Alana had overcome such odds. She loved God with all her heart. She had helped so many people. How could God allow this terrible thing to happen—while the alcoholic driver, who had been arrested on three separate occasions for drunk driving, had only minor injuries? More people at Alana's funeral were having big doubts about God's goodness than were willing to admit it.

It seemed to Rob that a lot of people changed after Alana's death. Sure, they acted like they were the same...but they really weren't. Rob could tell. It was as though they'd never trust God quite the same way again.

1. Where was God when Alana died?

2. Why do bad people live and good people die?

3. Respond to this statement: Life is not fair.

4. In light of what happened to Alana, read and respond to Psalm 73:4-12 and Job 21:7-15.

?

WILD WOMAN

Teresa grew up on the poor side of town. Her mother was a kid herself when Teresa was born. While Teresa was growing up, her mother went through a string of men—drug dealers, alcoholics, or worse—so that Teresa never did know her father. For as long as she could remember, Teresa had to fend for herself. She learned how to survive on the streets—and she had learned, somehow, to survive abuse from her mother's boyfriends.

By the time Teresa turned 13, she wanted out of the ghetto, away from drugs and alcohol and gangs. Teresa's social worker had always held out the option of a foster home when and if she was ready—and at 13 she was ready.

Now, two years later in her foster home, Teresa was doing well in school and stayed away from her mother. A lot of troubled kids at school could sense Teresa's street smarts and wanted to hang with her. Yet despite this pressure to go back to her old lifestyle, she refused to give in. Even her mother pleaded with her to come back and help raise her little sisters.

It didn't make it any easier that the "good" kids on campus were a hard group to break into—kids who had stable homes, who planned for their futures. In fact, it took two years for Teresa to make friends with Katerina. They went to youth group together at Katerina's church. Teresa loved it, and even started going out with some of the guys in the group. Life was starting to look good for Teresa.

Then one night Katerina called, crying.

"What's the matter?" Teresa asked.

"There are a bunch of people at church who don't want you coming to youth group anymore. They think...they think you're...a...a bad influence."

"Why? Because I smoke?"

"It's more than smoking, Teresa. They don't like the way you dress. They say it's suggestive. Some people have complained about your language, too."

"But Katerina, I just became a Christian. I'm trying. They should have seen me a year ago!"

"Oh, I know," said Katerina. "But it's just that...well, even my parents are concerned about our friendship. And I mean, really, some of those people that hang around you are kind of scary."

Three weeks later Teresa left her foster home and returned to her old neighborhood. She never attended church again. No one knows what happened to her.

"It's easy to recognize a Christian. Christians act like Christians. When Jesus comes into your heart, you're a new person. You don't act like you did before you met Christ. On the other hand, if you still do what you know is wrong, then you aren't a Christian. It's that simple. People who accept Christ, but whose language doesn't change, whose bad habits don't change, whose friends don't change—face it, they simply aren't changed. Which means they aren't really Christians. Just look at the Bible. The people that followed Jesus changed, or else they didn't follow him."

Kevin, first-year Bible student

The Stats

Some threats to teen safety are the following injury-causing behaviors:

- ❑ 21.7% rarely or never use seat belts.
- ❑ 92.8% rarely or never wear helmets while riding bikes.
- ❑ 38.8% have been passengers with drunk drivers.
- ❑ 20% have carried a weapon in the last month.
- ❑ 38.7% have been in a physical fight in the last year.
- ❑ 8.7% attempted suicide.

U.S. News and World Report
October 7, 1996

By the Book...

Do you not know that the wicked will not inherit the kingdom of God? Do not be deceived: Neither the sexually immoral nor idolaters or adulterers nor male prostitutes nor homosexual offenders nor thieves nor the greedy nor drunkards nor slanderers nor swindlers will inherit the Kingdom of God. And that is what some of you were. But you were washed, you were sanctified, you were justified in the name of our Lord Jesus Christ and led by the Spirit of our God.

1 Corinthians 6:9-11

---

1. If Teresa had told you her story, what would you have said to her?

2. What do you think about the fact that Teresa still smoked, still dressed a little wild, and still used language that her church thought was inappropriate?

3. Suppose Teresa decides to confront the church. What would you advise her to say?

"The Bible doesn't forbid wine

—it says we should be moderate. It doesn't say word one about marijuana, and I believe marijuana is less harmful than wine. So I believe as long as you smoke it in moderation where it is legal to do so, no problem."

Larry, high school valedictorian

The Stats

About 42% of 17-year-olds know a drug dealer and could purchase marijuana. What percentage of kids have been encouraged to buy or share pot?

☒ 9% of all 12-year-olds.

☒ 16% of all 13-year-olds.

☒ 33% of all 14-year-olds.

☒ 49% of all 15-year-olds.

☒ 53% of all 16-year-olds.

☒ 58% of all 17-year-olds.

USA Today
November 5, 1996

By the Book...

Do not be yoked together with unbelievers. For what do righteousness and wickedness have in common? Or what fellowship can light have with darkness? Therefore come out from them and be separate, says the Lord.

2 Corinthians 6:14, 17

Everything is permissible for me—but not everything is beneficial.

1 Corinthians 6:12

MIDDLE-CLASS DRUG DEALERS

Both Tim and Darlene are Christians, both are active members of Young Life, both come from good homes—and both are drug dealers. And they don't believe they are doing anything wrong. They sell only marijuana, which they believe is about the same as alcohol—and besides, pot is now legal in some states for medicinal purposes. Kids at their school will buy marijuana anyway, Tim and Darlene figure, so it's not as if they're creating new drug addicts. Neither do the pair waste their profits on cars and clothes: they're saving for a college education.

But Tim and Darlene have a problem. Keith, their Young Life director, has asked them if the rumors he's heard are true—because if they are, he's going to the police. And he doesn't want them coming to Young Life anymore.

Tim and Darlene are nervous about the situation, mostly because it could cut into their college money. They've got blackmail material, though—some of the Young Life kids are their best customers. Not to mention the daughter of a prominent pastor in town.

So Tim and Darlene admit to Keith that, yes, they deal marijuana. But they also explain why they don't think it's wrong. And finally, they tell Keith, if he says anything to the police, they'll reveal not only where they sell (before and after Young Life meetings), but also some interesting names from their customer list.

1. What are Keith's options? What would you do if you were Keith?

2. Based on this story, what are your impressions of Tim and Darlene?

3. What do you think of Tim and Darlene's arguments in defense of dealing pot?
   - "Kids are going to buy it anyway"
   - "It is already legal in some states, under certain conditions"
   - "They need the money for college"

4. Can you be a Christian and smoke marijuana? Can you be a Christian and sell marijuana?

THE BATTLE OVER HOME SCHOOL

The youth group had become a war zone—between the home-school kids and the "regular" school kids. The split between the two groups had gradually deepened during the previous four years, and now the home-school kids were a well-fortified clique within the youth group. They acted as though the rest of the kids were second-class Christians, as though the public-school kids had leprosy or AIDS or some kind of communicable disease that would contaminate the godly, pure, and spiritual home schoolers.

The result? At every meeting, every discussion—any youth group activity, even parties—the home schoolers would find a way to make an issue out of something, and it would inevitably turn into a huge problem. Worse, now even some parents were suggesting that the home schoolers have a separate youth group.

1. Is home schooling more Christian than public schooling? Or is public schooling more Christian than home schooling?

2. How relevant to your answer is this prayer by Jesus: "My prayer is not that you take them out of the world but that you protect them from the evil one" (John 17:15).

3. What is the difference between students who have been home schooled and those who have not?

4. What is there about home schooling that would make a home-schooled Christian student feel superior? What is there about attending a public school that would make a Christian student there feel superior?

"Home-schooled

kids are weird. They think the world is their enemy and Satan is hiding behind every bush. Most of them are way behind the kids in public schools, and they're completely clueless about television, cyberspace, the media...you know, the real world. What makes them really obnoxious is they act like they're so pure and we're so impure. Home school just isn't a good idea, once you see that most home schoolers are religious fanatics."

Kirsten, 17, junior

The Stats

◻ Home schoolers are increasing by 25% annually.

◻ The U.S. Department of Education says there's more than 500,000 participants and 1.2 million home-schooling advocates.

◻ All states allow home schooling, with California and Texas having the most home schoolers.

◻ In more than 65 studies, home schoolers performed at average or above-average levels on standardized testing, according to the president of the National Home Education Research Institute.

◻ Many colleges accept portfolios of home schoolers' work.

U.S. News & World Report
February 12, 1996

By the Book...

Consequently, you are no longer foreigners and aliens, but fellow citizens with God's people and members of God's household, built on the foundation of the apostles and prophets, with Christ Jesus himself as the chief cornerstone. In him the whole building is joined together and rises to become a holy temple in the Lord. And in him you too are being built together to become a dwelling in which God lives by his Spirit.
Ephesians 2:19-22

By this all men will know that you are my disciples, if you love one another.
John 13:35

Only Thing to Fear is Fear Itself

The Stats

Kids are increasingly scared these days—frightened to the point of losing their chances for productive and healthy futures. And they just may have valid reasons for these fears, according to a Gallup poll:

☒ 28% of teens say they know peers who have carried or regularly carry guns and knives to school.

☒ A quarter fear for their safety in school.

☒ Other fears include drug and alcohol abuse, violence, suicide, pregnancy, and AIDS.

Youthworker Update
September 1996

By the Book...

There is no fear in love. But perfect love drives out fear.

1 John 4:18a

It was another typical day at North Raleigh High School: three fights, one arrest for possession of a firearm, and the usual drug-sniffing dogs making their rounds along the lockers. As far as Lauren was concerned, school wasn't fun anymore.

Which was ironic. After all, she was the one who refused to attend the private school her parents wanted her to go to. She said she didn't believe Christians ought to hide from the real world. She wanted to be in a public school with her friends in the real world, she declared, instead of in some exclusive private school where everyone was protected from the "the world's" influence.

But Lauren's mind had changed. After history two guys followed her to her locker, then came up on both sides of her.

"Hey, babe...how come you're so stuck up, huh? We think we ought to spend some time together...or are you too good for us? Think about it, —we know where you live."

Lauren was petrified. Now she realized what she had been experiencing all year—not anxiety, not stress, but fear. She was afraid every day at school. No one ought to live like that, she told herself.

She ended up asking a friend to drive her home. That night Lauren asked her parents to transfer her to a private school.

A month later, if you had caught her between classes in her new private school, she would have told you it was the best decision she had ever made.

1. Is fear really that big of an issue in high schools today?

2. Is it wrong to not want to live in fear all the time?

3. Why didn't Lauren trust Psalm 121?
   I lift up my eyes to the hills—where does my help come from? My help comes from the Lord, the Maker of heaven and earth. He will not let your foot slip—he who watches over you will not slumber...
   The Lord will keep you from all harm—he will watch over your life; The Lord will watch over your coming and going both now and forevermore.

4. Is it wrong for Christians to fear?

5. Do you agree with Lauren's decision to change schools?

Youth Specialties Titles

Professional Resources

Administration, Publicity, & Fundraising (Ideas Library)
Developing Student Leaders
Equipped to Serve: Volunteer Youth Worker Training Course
Help! I'm a Junior High Youth Worker!
Help! I'm a Sunday School Teacher!
Help! I'm a Volunteer Youth Worker!
How to Expand Your Youth Ministry
How to Speak to Youth...and Keep Them Awake at the Same Time
One Kid at a Time: Reaching Youth through Mentoring
A Youth Ministry Crash Course
The Youth Worker's Handbook to Family Ministry

Youth Ministry Programming

Camps, Retreats, Missions, & Service Ideas (Ideas Library)
Compassionate Kids: Practical Ways to Involve Your Students in Mission and Service
Creative Bible Lessons in John: Encounters with Jesus
Creative Bible Lessons in Romans: Faith on Fire!
Creative Bible Lessons on the Life of Christ
Creative Junior High Programs from A to Z, Vol. 1 (A–M)
Creative Meetings, Bible Lessons, & Worship Ideas (Ideas Library)
Crowd Breakers & Mixers (Ideas Library)
Drama, Skits, & Sketches (Ideas Library)
Dramatic Pauses
Facing Your Future: Graduating Youth Group with a Faith That Lasts
Games (Ideas Library)
Games 2 (Ideas Library)
Great Fundraising Ideas for Youth Groups
More Great Fundraising Ideas for Youth Groups
Great Retreats for Youth Groups
Greatest Skits on Earth
Greatest Skits on Earth, Vol. 2
Holiday Ideas (Ideas Library)
Hot Illustrations for Youth Talks
More Hot Illustrations for Youth Talks
Incredible Questionnaires for Youth Ministry
Junior High Game Nights
Kickstarters: 101 Ingenious Intros to Just about Any Bible Lesson
Memory Makers
More Junior High Game Nights
Play It! Great Games for Groups
Play It Again! More Great Games for Groups
Special Events (Ideas Library)
Spontaneous Melodramas
Super Sketches for Youth Ministry

Teaching the Bible Creatively
Up Close and Personal: How to Build Community in Your Youth Group
Wild Truth Bible Lessons
Worship Services for Youth Groups

Discussion Starter Resources

Discussion & Lesson Starters (Ideas Library)
Discussion & Lesson Starters 2 (Ideas Library)
4th-6th Grade TalkSheets
Get 'Em Talking
High School TalkSheets
High School TalkSheets: Psalms and Proverbs
Junior High TalkSheets
Junior High TalkSheets: Psalms and Proverbs
Keep 'Em Talking!
More High School TalkSheets
More Junior High TalkSheets
What If..? 450 Thought-Provoking Questions to Get Teenagers Talking, Laughing, and Thinking
Would You Rather..? 465 Provocative Questions to Get Teenagers Talking

Clip Art

ArtSource Vol. 1—Fantastic Activities
ArtSource Vol. 2—Borders, Symbols, Holidays, and Attention Getters
ArtSource Vol. 3—Sports
ArtSource Vol. 4—Phrases and Verses
ArtSource Vol. 5—Amazing Oddities and Appalling Images
ArtSource Vol. 6—Spiritual Topics
ArtSource Vol. 7—Variety Pack
ArtSource Vol. 8—Stark Raving Clip Art
ArtSource CD-ROM (contains Vols. 1-7)

Videos

EdgeTV
The Heart of Youth Ministry: A Morning with Mike Yaconelli
Next Time I Fall in Love Video Curriculum
Understanding Your Teenager Video Curriculum

Student Books

Grow For It Journal
Grow For It Journal through the Scriptures
Wild Truth Journal for Junior Highers